A GIFT
FROM DANIEL

A GIFT
FROM DANIEL

Karen Alexander

A Perigee Book

The purpose of this book is not to dispense medical advice nor prescribe the use of any technique as a form of treatment for physical or mental problems without the advice of a physician either directly or indirectly. Neither the author nor the publisher can assume any responsibility for the use of information contained in this book.

A Perigee Book
Published by The Berkley Publishing Group
200 Madison Avenue
New York, NY 10016

Portions of this book were originally published in the author's fictionalized account of these events under the title *Losing Your Mind*, copyright © 1995 by Windover Press.

Copyright © 1996 by Karen Alexander
Book design by Rhea Braunstein
Cover design by James R. Harris
Cover photograph by Jan Tove Johansson/MASTERFILE

First edition: December 1996

Published simultaneously in Canada.

The Putnam Berkley World Wide Web site address is http://www.berkley.com/berkley

Library of Congress Cataloging-in-Publication Data
Alexander, Karen.
  A gift from Daniel / Karen Alexander.—1st ed.
    p. cm.
  "A Perigee book."
  ISBN 0-399-52244-1
  1. Alexander, Karen. 2. Spiritual biography—United States.
3. Private revelations. I. Title.
BL73.A54A3 1996
291.4'092—dc20
[B]   96-15438
                                                          CIP

Printed in the United States of America

10 9 8 7 6 5 4 3 2 1

‿❦ PREFACE ❦‿

Falling now, radiant love, its spinning threads of light compelled from the darkness. Fed by endless fountains of delight, sent forth with all that is needed, you are never alone, never forgotten and always, there is a whisper—my encouragement, my gratitude.

You are my creation, my thought, my heart. Into you I pour all of my hope, forever and ever. For it is you who will bring what I need to take us both home. And all around us, sparkling particle by particle, others spin in the darkness, and light comes into form. And they are filled then with purpose and infinite love, even as Gaia's body and boundless love bring forth all her creatures.

And when it is time, I will call you back into myself and receive from you the treasure you hold. I will embrace you, even as I do now. Then you will hear again all the love of the soul, and feel again the caress of my hand. You will gather my tears of joy, and dissolve into my heart—one forever with all that is.

I sing to you, my precious creation, my beloved servant. Take from me your life and all my courage. Receive from me all of what you will need, and do for me what I wish. For your deepest desire is what I also long for. Together, joined and blended, dancing light to light, we will leave the darkness forever behind. We will enter into the union from which we came.

Do not be afraid. For as much as the heart beats now in your chest, as much as the air flows into your body, so I am with you always. Lift up not your eyes and ears, for these are only needed to make your way in your Earthtime explorations. But free the strands of light which make your heart, and reach these up into the darkness. There in the stillness, you will feel my touch. And then, entwined, you will fill with me and know me. And there will be no end, for there is no separation but that which is made by confusion and ignorance.

And sing without ceasing to our sister Gaia as her gentle lullaby comforts you, as her creations nourish your sojourn in the Earthtime. For it is forever a circle of love . . . it always has been . . . and always will be.

Come, come my cherished creation. Come into your purpose, come into alignment, come into knowing who you are . . . and from this place, never be alone. Never be again lost in the darkness. Falling now, glorious spinning light, filled with love, birthed into being . . . you are forever and ever mine.

A Gift
from Daniel

꩜ ONE ꩜

Barely seat-back high, the bobbing spray of blond hair moved slowly down the aisle. Everything went into slow motion as the flight attendant bent over, read his ticket, and turned toward me. I tried to look away, but, with radar accuracy, she had already locked on. Her left arm rose and straightened, the index finger extending its deadly aim. Without sympathy, she pronounced my sentence: "Right there next to that lady." The words met my mind with the sensation of teeth biting into aluminum foil and the muscles in the back of my neck went into permanent gridlock.

Why me? I had been within a breath of having an empty seat next to me for the flight. Bone-tired, I had looked forward to the safety of the airplane as a tiny refuge from responsibility. Now I had been condemned to a siege of discomfort, strapped in without my permission next to a seven-year-old. I wondered how I could stay clear of an endless conversation with this kid.

"Can I sit by the window?" he asked sweetly.

"No!" I blurted. Exhaustion revealed itself in rudeness. Uncomfortably, I looked over at this little boy. His eyes were an astonishing clear blue. Set in a whimsical face, translucent white skin glowing under the wayward blond hair, those eyes were still, calm, and peaceful.

As I gazed at him, I decided to recant my former edict. "You can have the window seat. Nothing out there to see on this flight anyway."

"That's the best time to look," he replied, his little voice containing an enthusiasm suited to flying over Disneyland.

Strange kid, I thought. He'll probably talk nonstop, incessantly commenting on everything and anything, an endless source of useless noise, the kind with enough variety you can't ever get used to it to the point of blocking it out.

My friends have children like this. They have provided me with a colorful collection of reasons never to have children. I like children, other people's children, in other people's homes for very short periods of time with absolutely nothing blocking the door when I decide it's time for me to go. And don't leave me alone with any of them. Nearly every conversation I've ever had with a child goes like this:

"Hi. What's your name?"

Silence.

"How old are you?"

Silence.

"Do you go to school?"

Silence.

"Do you like school?"

Silence.

This effort is always followed by an interminable period during which the child continues to look at me, still silently, but with new unspoken judgment and an edge of pity because I cannot for the life of me figure out anything else to say. When his mother or father finally returns, my heart surges, suddenly full of gratitude normally reserved for being rescued at sea after ten days without food or water.

Then the noise starts. With a mysterious invisible "on" switch tripped magically by a parent entering the room, this sphinx bursts to life at volume ten. Suddenly, he can't stop talking and jumping up and down. Feeling like the target of a hysterical cat, I try to release myself from the confusion of arms and legs grabbing at my body. I need to back up for a minute, develop a plan. Not possible. The child gathers reinforcements, toys with names and purposes I've never heard of, and explanations in fragments that sound like what comes out of a radio when the dial is turned too fast.

The little voice broke through my ruminations. "My name is Daniel." Guileless eyes were fixed upon my face, waiting for an answer.

Here we go, I thought. "I'm Karen," I replied quietly.

"Yep, you are." He offered this curious statement with an element of appreciation in his voice. I caught myself looking at this little boy wearing a bright blue T-shirt tucked neatly into gray sweat pants. His high-top sneakers looked well used, and now bumped together with a syncopated rhythm that meant something only to him.

Our plane's engines began to whine, and we moved slowly backward. I felt a surge of responsibility. "Put your seat belt on." I couldn't just ignore him all the way to Seattle.

We sat at the end of the runway, and it seemed impossible that this plane could ever make it off the ground. I thought about a friend who told me planes get into the air through the efforts of tiny, invisible, tribal strongmen; he called them "menehunes." Supposedly, they raced along beneath the wings, their bare feet pounding in powerful unison. At precisely the right instant, they would vault the giant mechanical beast into the sky. On every flight since he told me that story, I checked for them with one eye.

Maybe I should tell this child about the menehunes. I was willing to talk to him while we took off, even hold his hand if he wanted me to. "Are you scared about flying?" I asked.

"I like to fly," he answered brightly. "I fly all the time."

"By yourself?" He seemed so young to be traveling alone.

"Yep." He paused. "Well, nobody's ever really by themselves."

He's a confident little kid, I thought. Maybe one parent lives in Idaho and the other in Seattle.

"How many times have you flown?" I inquired.

"A bunch of times, and to lots of different places," he answered with a smile.

"How come you get to travel so much?" I asked, feeling a little envious. I loved to travel, but I was seventeen years old before I ever left California.

He responded with positive certainty. "Everybody can travel all over if they really want to."

That's it; he must be an airline kid. He can fly anywhere and thinks everyone can do it.

We were in the air! Finally, I was on my way to Seattle. Feeling excited and relieved, I began to mentally organize the flight. I had an excellent book, and there was always music on the headphones. Ah, maybe a wonderful, secret violation of the work ethic that ruled my life . . . a nap.

It was good to leave work behind, even for a few days. If I allowed myself to get tired enough, I began to feel that maybe the critics were right. Maybe psychotherapy couldn't really help anybody after all. I had certainly chalked up my share of success stories, and most of my new clients were coming from word of mouth, a good sign, but I still felt a certain dissatisfaction with my work.

I was adept at discovering the dynamics that had created my clients' symptoms. Initially, they would be impressed with these new cognitive insights into why they were depressed, anxious, had panic attacks, drank too much, couldn't sleep, or kept getting involved in the same dysfunctional relationship patterns. For a few sessions we would bask in the afterglow of these new revelations, and they would lavish me with praise for being such a great therapist.

But the enthusiasm would fade as we realized that, although they now understood perfectly why their lives had been plagued with symptoms, they still got depressed, felt anxious, had to fight off panic attacks, drank too much, tossed and turned all night, and continued to accept dinner invitations from people who were making alimony payments in six states. In the majority of cases, there seemed to be very little correlation between a client's intellectual understanding and anything really changing on the emotional level. This was especially true in the most complex cases. I wanted to do something more for those individuals who had suffered through a lifetime of mental anguish. I was touched by those whose eyes no longer held any light of hope. I didn't want to be just another shrink with another line, but my energy could not overcome the inertia of thirty years of pain that went soul-deep.

There had to be a better way. I could not bring myself to accept that certain individuals were destined to be permanently trapped in a private hell. People were being medicated at an alarming rate, and an artificial abatement of symptoms seemed to be accepted as an appropriate therapeutic goal. But I clung to the belief that recovery was not the psychological equivalent of growing a third arm. Surely, these suffering clients were not trying to do something against the natural order of life itself.

"Flying on an airplane sure takes a long time." The young voice broke into my painful thoughts.

"Yes, sometimes it does," I responded patiently. "We're flying all the way to Seattle, and that's a pretty long way. You know that, Daniel. You said you've flown lots of times."

He really was kind of cute. His face pressed up against the window, he seemed completely engrossed in watching the clouds underneath us. Maybe this flight wouldn't be so bad after all. I opened my book.

"Karen?" The soft voice found me once again. "Do you want to see some of the places I can go?" I glanced up to find eyes alert with expectation.

I supposed he had family travel pictures to show me. Surprisingly, I was curious to see where he had visited. "Okay Daniel, let's take a look at what you've got."

After releasing the seat belt, he wiggled himself down onto the floor. Wedged up against my leg, his little back strained as he pulled out a bright red backpack stashed under the seat ahead of him. I hadn't even noticed him putting it down there when he plunked beside me.

"Need some help?" I asked, reaching down for his bag.

Like a fisherman with an enormous catch on the line, he tugged away at his prize. "No, I can get it." Finally, he let out a big breath and pushed the bag up onto his seat.

"Do you want to see?" he asked, looking straight up at me.

"Sure, why not?"

"Do you want to see?" he repeated, strangely serious.

"Yes," I said, feeling impatient with the need to repeat myself.

"Karen, you have to want to see," he said gently. Somehow, the little voice slipped inside me. Sparkling eyes locked with mine, and the small hand reached out and touched my face. A sensation of overwhelming love coursed through me. It was an odd sort of love, more like unbearable compassion combined with great joy.

Lost for a moment in this exquisite rush of feeling, I closed my eyes. I was floating, drifting on a river in a summertime of my childhood. I was settled into an inner tube, hot sun on my legs, a glittering collection of tiny drops of cool water falling in slow motion. . . . I was in heaven.

Love: how desperate we are to find it, experience it, and own it. And once found, it so quickly dies inside its cage of expectations and failed dreams. How angry we are when it cannot survive its imprisonment. We grieve. What we needed most has died at our own hands. Then we begin to hunt again for this elusive requirement for survival. But what I felt was different. This was wonderful, so innocent, so clearly beyond containment.

Abruptly, energy shot through my body, and the astounding peace was replaced by a fervor, a passion. Like an electrical current it surged up from my feet through my legs, urgently moving without restraint. This power inside insisted its way into my chest, entered my heart, and erupted in feelings I did not know I could have. My eyes sprung open to find the child who had brought me to such a place within myself.

The blue eyes were there, filled now with amusement.

The plane was gone.

ঙ TWO ঙ

In the distance, I could see the silver tail of the 737 disappearing into a bank of soft, gray clouds. My mind buckled like a piece of cardboard held up to a strong wind. Instinctively, I began pumping my arms and legs wildly, flapping like a strange, spasmodic bird.

The plane's gone! It's not here! The voice inside my head screamed like a heavy-metal singer into his microphone. Think. Think. Think. Think. I'm going to die. The plane's gone. What do you mean, think? The goddamn plane is gone. I'm going to fall. I'm going to die.

Beyond the frenzy of my arms, I saw the little boy. Peacefully standing there, he said quietly, "You don't need to do that. Everything's okay."

I shouted in terror. "Everything's okay?! The plane's gone. There . . . is . . . no . . . plane. We've lost everything. We're going to fall!" Think. Think. Think. There is no plane and I'm trying to convince a seven-year-old that it's important!

"Look around," he said, amusement now in his voice. "Are we falling?"

A wailing noise came from my mouth. "Of course we're falling. There is no plane. Without the plane, we fall. . . ."

"Karen, are we falling?" The little voice was so quiet, so comfortable.

I made myself look down and saw gray mist shifting silently

around my legs and feet. I wasn't going anywhere. My head whipped up in astonishment. "What the hell is going on?"

The little boy giggled, his face demonstrating a child's honesty at seeing something he finds absolutely hysterical. His musical laughter filled the silence, and I felt the mist surround my body and play across my face. Gratefully, I took in the beautiful fragrance of raindrops early in the morning.

I loved playing in the rain. Where I grew up, it had come rarely. When dark, pregnant clouds filled the sky, I would hope with all my heart they would deliver their promise. Then I'd fly out of the house to jump in every puddle I could find, laughing and laughing. Even when the mud splashed up and covered my clothes, I'd keep jumping, although I knew my mom would be mad. The harder it would rain, the happier I would get. Our neighbor, Mr. Henderson, would yell through his screen door, "Girl! Don't you know enough to get out of the rain?" I did. But I also knew I needed to stay out in the rain.

Somehow, the rain replenished my soul. Everything would seem new: the trees, my neighborhood, my house, even me. Clean, free, clear, we all had a new start. I'd come in only when some adult would finally intrude on my bliss. Even after the obligatory hot bath, I would stand by the window and watch the raindrops pass by the streetlight on their way to Earth and wonder who had sent them.

"Are you coming?" Daniel had stopped giggling and was looking at me intently.

"What?" I managed to choke. My body was no longer fighting to prevent a fall. But go somewhere? My mind struggled to find an explanation for what was happening and came to the only obvious conclusion. This had to be an absolutely terrifying dream.

Wake up! This is one of those awful falling dreams where you topple from a building and wake up just before you hit the pavement. Everyone has dreams like that. Just like the one where you look down and find yourself naked in a restaurant or the one that has the phone that won't work in an emergency. Regular, bad dreams. This was a complex one of those. Okay. Wake up!

"Are you coming?" Daniel spoke again. God, he seemed so real. And the taste of the clouds. So real . . . wake up!

"You said you wanted to see where I can go. . . ." The little boy's voice reminded me of my statement with a kind of positive neutrality. Just a fact, a gentle reminder.

"Okay, Daniel, I don't understand what's happening here." God, I'm talking to a hallucination. That's it—some sort of horrible drug had gotten into my system. How could that have happened? I don't take drugs. I missed the sixties. I've never taken drugs.

Daniel spoke again. "Karen, it's either important or it's not. You have to decide . . . are you coming?" He turned and started to move away. Hallucination or not, I didn't want him to leave me.

"Okay, okay, I'll come," I sputtered.

The most beautiful smile I had ever seen changed the little face into a beacon of joy; he was so happy. Actually, he was ecstatic. "That's good." was all he said, but it felt like a blessing.

I had heard the best thing to do with a bad trip is to try to relax and not fight it. If you accept that you're helplessly along for the ride, it is a lot easier. If I could just get myself off the plane in Seattle, I would go to a good hotel and wait it out. Eat, rest, and forget this bizarre thing ever happened to me.

"Daniel." I tried to steady myself. "Daniel, where are we going? How are we going to get there?"

The joyful smile still on his face, he replied softly, "It's easy. All you have to do is remember who you are."

"Who I am?" I've been trying to figure that out my whole life.

I guess it starts in school. "Who are you?" is really "What can you do?" The system is set up to reveal who is competent and skilled and who is not. Who learns to tell time first? Who has the best spelling test? Who can add and subtract better? There are layers and layers of this method of classifying human beings.

Kids arrive at school with family beliefs entrenched: "You're just like your uncle Fred." "Everyone in our family has always been good at this." "A Smith doesn't think like that." "Honey, you won't ever be good at math." "Don't waste your time like that, let me show you how it's done." "You're the kind of kid who will grow up to be a teacher." I spent a lot of time helping my clients break free of the things they had learned about themselves that were untrue. I strongly believed most things could be changed with determined willingness. But who did the person really set out to become?

I emerged from my thoughts as Daniel said quite seriously, "Karen, you must remember who you are."

I didn't know what he wanted from me. "Okay. I am Karen Alexander." That sounded silly. Of course I could remember my name. What was the point?

"Well . . ." Mist drifted past the little hallucination's face, and I impatiently waited for him to explain. "Karen is the name of your body and the name of what you do, but that's not who you are."

Feeling agitated at his answer to a question I did not even understand, I snapped, "Daniel, just what do you mean?" I was ready to leave this dream world. I'd had enough. But Daniel's eyes danced with a loving humor that only increased my aggravation.

"Just tell me what you mean or help me get out of here."

There. I had asked the product of my hallucination to help me out of the hallucination. That was scary.

He looked at me with renewed intensity. "You haven't been drugged, you know."

How did he do that? "How did you know what I was thinking?"

"It's easy," he said, grinning. "You just have to remember who it is that you really are."

"I give up." How was I going to figure out what he wanted from me? I might as well let him answer his own question. "All right . . . who am I?"

"You have to remember, not ask somebody else," he said with a shrug of his small shoulders. "If you ask other people, all you end up with is their ideas about who they think you are and who they want you to be. What good is that?"

I took the bait. "I've always been independent!" I didn't like the idea of being a social construct. "I've worked on myself a lot. I can tell you who I am."

"Okay . . . tell me," he replied, his face open and accepting.

"All right." I took a deep breath. "My name is Karen Alexander. I grew up in Santa Barbara, California, but now I live in Boise, Idaho. I'm married and I don't have any children. I have a nice home and two dogs. I have a master's degree in counseling and another one in public administration. I'm a successful therapist who works primarily with survivors of abuse. I'm healthy and strong. Let's see, what else? I love to travel, I like to give workshops, I have good friends." I finished, feeling somewhat smug at the excellent presentation of my life, and looked over at Daniel.

"Well, that's good!" He paused and smiled gently at me. "That's all important stuff, but who acquired it?"

Acquired. The word stopped my mind. For one thing, it was a big word for such a small person to use, but that wasn't what bothered me. It was that particular word. To "acquire" means that you have to do something to get something. It's a word that describes action. His statement implied the existence of something that acted in order to be, or have, all of the things I had talked about. That was an odd thought.

I spoke slowly. "Daniel . . . are you saying that there's some part of me that I don't know about that decided to acquire all the stuff I just described? There's a part of me that all the rest of this belongs to?"

The little-boy smile was back. "Yep. That's it. You just forget when you're on Earth, so now you have to remember who you are!"

I was considering what he said and getting ready to ask another question when he disappeared, his wind-chime laugh fading quickly into complete silence.

ꕥ THREE ꕥ

"Daniel, wait . . . wait! What do I do? Where do I go? I can't remember!" Turning around, I could find no sign of the child. Suspended in the clouds, I was completely alone.

Think. Think. Think. The plane is gone. I'm out here with no one to help me. Where was that little boy? My mind pounded like forced labor in a quarry, working to convince me I was suffering from drug ingestion. He's not a hallucination, another part of me argued back. But what else could he be?

Whatever he is, I decided, I've got to find him. Without him, I'll never get back. Back to where? The plane, the ground, sanity? How could he leave me out here like this? What was I saying? How could I be out here? Something deep inside me began to suggest that while finding Daniel was urgent, it had to do with going forward and not back.

Think. Think. Think. What do you do when you're lost? Stop and think. I looked around as wispy white clouds went by. Where could he have gone?

"Daniel!" I yelled as loud as I could. Nothing. He was my escort through this strange experience. How would I survive without him? This wasn't the kind of thing you do by yourself.

I had seen so many clients who were afraid of flying. Some were worried about a crash, others obsessed by the fact that only a piece of metal kept them from a deathly fall. But here I was, suspended in the air. The clouds floated around me, separating to accommodate my presence. I didn't seem to be going anywhere.

"Come on, Daniel, tell me how to do this! Tell me what to do!" I shouted in frustration.

Having no choice, I decided to try to answer his question. I am . . . I am . . . I am what? I don't know, damn it! I need help here! Help from whom? The only one who could help me was me, I thought. But I'm just a person who was contentedly riding along in an airplane. Now I'm out here! I should be falling and I'm not. Who is it that's not falling? It can't be me as I know me; that would be impossible.

"Tell me!" I bellowed. "Tell me who I am!" Suddenly, everything changed.

The clouds were gone, replaced by a vast, empty darkness. Glittering stars far, far away made my loneliness seem infinite. Faintly hoping to find Daniel behind me, I turned around. My breathing stopped, as I was paralyzed by the sight of an exquisite blue sphere rotating slowly in the silence.

Earth.

ᘓ FOUR ᘔ

"Ladies and gentlemen, this is your captain speaking. Out the left side of the airplane you can see . . ." I peeled myself off the ceiling of the plane, my heart pounding, adrenaline bursting in every cell of my body.

"Jesus!" I blurted. The woman in the seat across the aisle was silent, but she gave me a smug look. She seemed to take pleasure in watching another human being reenter waking reality at supersonic speed. Trembling, I deliberately slowed my breathing and worked to gain control of my turbulent emotions.

"Hi!" Happy eyes found mine, and the little boy's face broke into a big grin. He had his tray table down, and several books with bright covers were stacked in front of him. "I really like this one a lot," he said enthusiastically. "It's a really, really good story. Want to read it?"

I stared at him, at once confused and extremely grateful to find myself back to normal. Back from where? What a terrible dream, an absolute nightmare. The little hand still held the favorite book out to me. I felt afraid to touch it, afraid to get lost again. God, it had felt so real. I closed my eyes for a second.

"Would you like something to drink, Miss?" I tracked the voice before cracking my eyes just wide enough to see a flight attendant.

"Something to drink?" she repeated.

"Uh, yes . . . yes, that would be good." I needed something to soothe my nerves a little, quiet my mind.

"What would you like?" Her cheerfulness was reassuring. Whenever I got nervous on an airplane, I always looked at the flight attendants to see if they were all right. If they continued to smile, I would relax.

Random thoughts ricocheted through my head. Everything had been so vivid only a moment ago. It seemed strange that I should have to speak my words. Couldn't she just hear them? Didn't she know what I needed? But this was the real world. People stand and stare at you when you don't answer.

"I'll take a scotch and soda."

The words sounded strange coming out of my mouth. I had always felt that people who knew immediately what they wanted to drink must drink frequently. If you hunted around and said something like, "Well, let's see, I'll have a . . . no . . . gee . . . what sounds good? I can never think of anything . . . oh, maybe . . . do you have any white wine . . . a small glass . . ." This meant that you seldom drank.

"That will be three dollars," she said as she lowered my tray table.

I handed her three one-dollar bills and thought of my father. When I was little, he showed me how to fold a dollar bill back upon itself lengthwise and make George Washington's endless forehead meet the top of his high-necked white shirt so he looked like a giant toadstool. I had repeated this magical transformation to countless audiences; it was always a sort of private tribute to my father.

I sipped my drink and wondered how they made the tubular ice cubes with holes in the middle. I remembered the promises I had made to myself in the middle of the nightmare. I would check into that wonderful hotel and enjoy myself, forget the whole thing.

I love the endless stream of hot water provided by a hotel shower. I sometimes sit on the floor of the shower and let the water run over me. If you plug your ears, the sound of the water on your skull is amplified. With my eyes closed and the lights off, I would imagine myself soaked in a wonderful storm with magically warm rain. This activity has become almost sacred. Responsibilities and problems do not exist as the warm, thundering water caresses me and moves me beyond the limits of time and space to the greatest privacy that can be found.

Finally, I turned back toward Daniel and took the book. Maybe it would help to read a story to a real little boy . . . make the feelings left over from my terrible dream go away.

Daniel looked at me expectantly. How simple he was. I could make his whole day just by giving my attention and taking the time to read a story. I looked into the innocent, open face. He was so totally present with me, his mind nowhere else but right on me. I was the center of his world at this moment, the sun all the planets must ask for directions. And yet he was far from empty. This little person seemed filled with intelligence and hope, courage and dedication to being alive.

What happens to us? How does all of that get replaced with such heaviness? I couldn't imagine what could happen in my own life that would bring me the level of happiness I saw in Daniel's face at the simple prospect of having a story read to him. Where did it go, that part of me? I know how to enjoy myself as well as the next person, but this was pure. It didn't have anything at all to do with impressing somebody or getting something. It had nothing to do with winning or protecting secrets or keeping an image up. I thought of my attempts at conversation with other kids. No wonder they had never worked. I didn't really care what school they went to, and they knew that. I didn't care about making real contact with them, and they knew that, too. The pity in their eyes . . . what else could be felt watching somebody work so hard to avoid being herself?

Be yourself. Easy to say and hard to do. Daniel wanted to be noticed, but as himself, not as an image he produced for me. All he wanted was some company in his own existence. He offered an invitation to join with him as he was. Simple.

I thought about my close relationships. "Close" seemed to translate into time spent doing something with other people. I have shopping friends, go-to-lunch friends, workout friends. We talk about people we know and what we've been doing, not how hard it can be sometimes to just keep going. We never mention how demoralizing it is to realize that you're so afraid of making someone unhappy, you have to invent "what's right," and it might have nothing to do with what you want or who you really are. We don't talk about the fear of not making it, of ending up with nothing and no one.

I used to know what I wanted, what felt good and what didn't. I knew the people I wanted to be with and the ones I didn't. There were no social requirements. I never even had to say "hi" to anyone, even if they said it to me. I remember when my days were spent sitting in a tall tree watching the birds zoom in and out, when a burst of yellow butterflies was enough to send elation into my heart. I can remember being real. What happens to us?

"Are you going to read?" I was no longer resentful about my company on the flight. I had not read a children's book since I was small. There was a place in me that seemed happy about reading a story, a place I had forgotten about.

I sighed. "Yes, I'd like to read the book, Daniel. It looks like a good one." As I turned it over, the title screamed in bold orange letters: **Remember Who You Are.**

ॐ FIVE ॐ

"Where did you get this?" My voice sounded sharper than I had meant, but I was scared. "Remember who you are." That's what Daniel had said to me in the dream, right before he left me alone out there.

Ignoring my question, the little boy said, "Here, open it up. It's so cool." As his fingers pulled at the paper, he brought me face-to-face with an image that took my breath away. I stared down at the page. In front of me was the bright blue sphere and, slowly, it began to turn.

"See!" His voice was excited, happy, and far away. I looked up. Daniel stood twenty feet away from me. Twenty feet! The plane was gone again.

"Isn't this great?" His smile moved him closer. Beyond us, the Earth rotated in the darkness.

I managed to force words through the barricade of fear in my throat. "Oh, God, Daniel. What is happening to me?"

"You're doing better," he answered brightly. "You remembered you didn't have to try to fly!" Peals of laughter filled the quiet.

"You looked so funny before," he sputtered, "flapping your arms around." He was like any other kid, face turning red, gasping for air, over something he found hilarious.

Running out of patience, I cried, "Do you think this is easy?

Planes disappearing, finding out I can stand in space! One minute life is normal, the next it's crazy."

Daniel stopped laughing and looked toward the Earth. "Isn't she beautiful?" he said, his voice filled with emotion. Then, moving away from me, he announced, "Let's go. We have a lot to do."

"Go? Go where?" The last time he mentioned going somewhere, he left and I stayed. Fear flooded through me at the prospect of abandonment, and I pleaded, "Daniel, don't do the thing where you disappear and leave me out here again."

He looked at me strangely. "You still don't remember?"

"Please don't start that again," I replied irritably. "I don't remember who I am. I can't. Just tell me and get it over with." I stared at him indignantly and asked, "Who am I, Daniel? And don't leave me out here again to figure it out."

I refused to blink, thinking perhaps if I looked at him hard enough, this would all make sense. At least, if I kept him in my sight, he wouldn't vanish. The blue eyes locked with mine. We stared at each other like Jeffrey Collins and I used to do in the third grade. Life depended on not blinking first. The one who lost would suffer the judgment of the twenty-seven other kids who found the game so interesting. Clenched in ocular combat, the eyes would begin to burn and water. The classroom would blur and the body's command to blink would finally be obeyed by the tortured lids and down they would fall, all honor and pride descending with them. I wasn't going to blink this time. I didn't dare. The idea that Daniel could disappear again was too frightening.

"Okay," he said sweetly, blond lashes dipping past his eyes.

"Okay?" I was surprised and pleased, but totally unsure of what I had won.

"Okay. I'll tell you." He shrugged his shoulders and allowed his hands to fall together, looking like a miniature major league pitcher getting set to launch a fastball.

"Really?" Relief swept through me. "That's great. Okay, tell me."

"Actually, I have to show you," he replied with a smile. "That will work a lot better."

"Okay, fine. Show me." I had never liked relationship games that involved trying to guess what someone else knows. I was ready for him to show me.

What could "remember who you are" mean? Was he talking about reincarnation? I couldn't take that seriously. "What's your sign?" used to be everybody's ticket to conversation. Now it's "I was Marie Antoinette, who were you?" Nobody was ever a potato farmer who lived a normal life with a nice wife and six kids. These people are always an emperor or part of a harem or Christopher Columbus. In a few years, everyone will have been Elvis or Marilyn Monroe.

Beyond panic, I was now impatient. I was standing out in space, talking to a seven-year-old about things I didn't understand and feeling annoyed! I thought about how human beings make that transition. Things are only absolutely amazing for a short time, before we begin tearing apart the experience. We are constantly calling for the out-of-the-ordinary experience, but once we have it we attack with every cynical, intellectualizing weapon we have. Then we're disappointed. And we start the search again.

A Native American friend of mine once told me one of the reasons that most people don't have visions is that they insist they can't exist. We guard our rational ideas so well that nothing can disturb them. We forget that a vision couldn't break into such a mental prison even if it did exist. Then we have our evidence. Visions do not exist because I do not have them. I do not have them because I believe they do not exist.

Following the careful advice of a spiritual teacher, I went out to a supposedly magical place in the desert once and spent a whole day waiting for a vision. Nothing happened. But my mind had been on red alert, judging, watching, afraid at once that I would see something and that I would not see anything. I'm convinced that if I had seen something, that same mind would have found a quick method for explaining it away.

Is that what this was about? Was it some kind of vision about my life? Shouldn't there be a great chorus of angels, skies parting, God's deep, resonant voice? If God was trying to tell me something, surely it wouldn't be through a little boy. If God wants you to hear a special message, isn't it more formal than this? Wouldn't it come at church or in a prayer or something?

People spend lifetimes in churches, listening to ministers, burning candles, singing, offering communal prayers. That would seem the logical place to receive edicts from God, not out here with a giggling, illogical child.

But people don't hear anything directly from God in church either. If they did, the number of churchgoers would be going up, not down. Somehow, the idea that God would speak to a random congregation on a Sunday morning seemed highly unlikely. Of course, there were always reports of a statue crying somewhere in another country. But if God wanted to say something, why bother with forcing tears out of marble? Wouldn't He just say it?

I grew up in a regular Methodist church without crying statues or parting skies. I went to Sunday school where, under the watchful eyes of a blond, blue-eyed Jesus, we heard stories from the Bible, drew pictures, and sang songs. Once a month, we joined with the whole congregation in the sanctuary for regular services. Terribly bored, I entertained myself with the little pencils and pieces of paper mounted on the back of the pew in front of me. I would write messages to my friends, draw, make airplanes, anything to get through the endless combinations of words coming from the minister.

He stood up high, in a special box. Dressed in a billowy, white robe, he would talk of things I could not understand. He looked important. I knew that he had some kind of special relationship with God, but I didn't know what it was. Behind him was an enormous stained-glass window depicting Jesus with a bunch of little children and some sheep. I had heard that Jesus loved the little children, and I really liked the sheep. But the minister sounded mad a lot of the time. He commanded us to love Jesus, but I didn't understand how to love somebody I'd never even met. He talked about how much Jesus loved us and so we should love Him back. This was really confusing. The minister was angry because I couldn't love a person I didn't know who already loved me for some mysterious reason.

And then, after all the words about love, suddenly this stirred-up authority would command us to "Eat the body and drink the blood of Christ." I didn't even want to eat the sheep, let alone this person who supposedly loved me.

I grew to hate those excursions to the sanctuary. I tried to ask about this strange exercise everyone was so willing to perform. I was told "We do this because we love Jesus." Back to that again.

As I got older and could grasp the idea of symbolism, of course the horror went out of this communal practice. But I still didn't understand it very well. When I asked for assistance, what came back was an explanation that didn't make sense to me, or more often, a crisp admonition that I didn't yet have a close enough relationship with Jesus to understand Him. If I would only love Him more, I would understand everything. There we were again. How do I love someone I can't understand and whom I've never met?

"Pray," adults would suggest.

Prayer always seemed like a strange idea to me. Besides, the things people asked for were often ridiculous. They would try to gain God's attention so He would bestow good favor on them and they could win a baseball game or get a new house. I had known people who prayed to God for everything, like placing an order at McDonald's, picking it up at the second window. God couldn't really be some kind of clerk, taking requests and filling them at random. Everybody who went off to war prayed for safety and victory. Didn't the God of the enemy listen to them? What about when it was supposed to be the same God, Christians against Christians or Moslems against Moslems?

Prayer. That's one of those things you're supposed to know how to do. Everyone around you seems to have it down. Of course, I know how to look serious and bow my head. But what to do with the hands seems open for debate. Once, I went to a Catholic church with a friend. It was intimidating . . . all the kneeling and half-kneeling and sort of kneeling and getting prepared to kneel. Anyway, I would close my eyes and talk to God inside my head and say "Amen" and get up with roughly the same emotional impact as watering my house plants.

Well into adolescence, I decided to accept the judgment of my minister. According to him, I didn't appreciate the love Jesus offered, and so I was doomed. But doomed to what? The Methodist church was never clear about that. I did learn that God was out there somewhere, and He was undoubtedly very angry with me. Was it now time for me to meet God and get my well-deserved punishment?

"Well, are you coming?" Daniel's voice felt like an electrical shock.

"Coming where?" I stammered, more than half convinced I was about to meet my Maker. After all, God was the only one who could be behind my situation.

"Coming with me so I can show you who you are." His words were full of impatience.

"Daniel . . ." I was afraid to form the rest of my question. "Are we going to see God?"

Exploding with laughter, he finally managed to wheeze out, "Of course not!"

"What is so funny?" I demanded, feeling insulted.

Through his laughter, I heard him say, "Why would anyone have to go see God?"

໑ SIX ໑

After thirty-eight years of what my Sunday school teacher would describe as "rebellion against God," I was finally admitting I would need to face Him. For decades, I had expanded my capacity to avoid the inevitable. Now I was ready, and this child found it hysterical.

Actually, I was far from ready. Who is ready? If you told the average person she would meet God in an hour, nobody would be ready. Everyone has some vague idea about what God expects. And we all know we haven't come anywhere near that. So we put it off. We will think about it later, much later, when we're old—even better, when we're dying. It's definitely a "someday" proposition.

Even if you go to church every Sunday, you still screw it up. Going to church just reminds you of it more often. Not that I'm a terrible person. I've always thought I was a good person, but not good enough to meet God.

Meet God . . . oh, my God . . . what would it mean? This is the day I will have to look at my whole life in excruciating detail and explain, one by one, my failings. Why didn't I do a better job? Why didn't I get any warning it was going to be today of all days? A woman should have a chance to prepare for an audience with God. I'm not even dressed appropriately.

"Oh, God!" I gulped hard, and wondered if all of those verbal indiscretions would be forgiven. The Ten Commandments . . . I couldn't remember what they were, but I was fairly sure I had done pretty well with those. I never killed anyone. My mother and father were happy with the way I had treated them. That was two; what about the other eight?

Maybe God would be like He is in all those paintings from the Renaissance: big, bearded, angry, powerful. I was starting to panic. What would happen to me when God really took a good look at my life?

Maybe there really was a hell. The proselytizers who had rung my doorbell at profoundly inconvenient times on equally inconvenient days were sure of it. If we didn't do precisely the right thing, we would be condemned to a terrible eternity. I actually invited them in once. After thirty minutes about the sins of mankind and the inevitable punishment coming from God, I had lost my patience and asked them to leave. They did, after dumping a load of unwelcome pamphlets on my coffee table. Maybe I should have read their material.

Daniel stood by my sleeve. "It's all right," he said softly. His face was gentle. He was no longer laughing, but amusement still played in his eyes. "Everything is perfectly all right."

"Daniel, please tell me what's going on." I was desperate for some answers. "I don't understand. I don't know where to go or what I'm supposed to do. Please tell me."

"Come with me," he replied quietly. "Come on . . . I'll show you."

Too tired to question him, I simply decided I would no longer fight. I would go with him and meet God. And with my decision, everything for me was forever changed.

❧ SEVEN ❧

"What . . . what are we doing here?" Hardly able to believe my eyes, I exclaimed, "Daniel, what are we doing in Boise, Idaho?"

I had grown to love this small city in the empty expanse of desert falling out from the Rocky Mountains. Beautiful wilderness rose up out of the barren sweep of sagebrush territory. Within minutes, you could find high mountains, big trees, and white water. Boise tended to be a good mile behind the trends from more sophisticated areas of the country. Like what happens when a rock is dropped into calm water, changes from the big cities would ripple toward me, and I could see them approaching from a long distance. That made it comfortable. I had a chance to get prepared, decide what I wanted to do before anything ever reached me.

Out of the corner of my eye, I saw Daniel walking away. "Wait. Wait!" I called.

Thankful to find that my legs worked just fine back on terra firma, I caught up with him. We were in a park—the same park in which I had played softball, languished by the duck pond, and flown my kite. It was a great park, but . . . "Daniel, I thought we were going to see God. What are we doing here? God's up, not down."

Daniel walked even faster, determination showing in his small, square jaw. I tried to get his attention. "How did we get here? Last thing I remember, we were in space. That's a long way. How did we get here so fast? Where are we going?"

We were approaching the little kids' play area. I could see a tiny girl with a spectacular smile and new red sneakers. With mom at one end and dad at the other, she was working up the courage to go down the slide. In this moment, her entire world was made up of that shiny, silver slide and two people who obviously adored her. Just like these kids, I used to ride the merry-go-round, swing high in the air, and race down the slide. It seemed like such an impossibly long time ago. Did Daniel want to go and play on the swings? Had we gotten off the airplane and come down from outer space so Daniel could ride on a swing?

I made another attempt to get an answer. "Daniel ... Daniel ... what are you doing?" His high-tops slid over the grass, and he headed for the playground equipment.

"Come on!" he said enthusiastically. Good. He had finally found his voice. "Let's play!"

I was amazed. "Daniel, we can't play now! We're on our way to see God." But he sloshed straight through the sand and climbed up on the monkey bars.

"See, this is fun! Come and play," he said, laughing.

"Daniel, this is serious." Frustration filled my words. "We have to do something really important. We don't have time to play."

"There's always time to play," he replied, pulling himself up higher.

"No, there is not always time to play," I said with the moral imperative of a grownup who thinks she knows everything. "You play after you do the things that are important."

He tipped himself over backward and hung upside down, an enormous smile filling his face. "See, there's always time to play, because play is important."

I wasn't sure whether that smile reflected pure pleasure at playing on the monkey bars, or was the result of having gotten the best of me. Crouching down, I turned my head at an awkward angle, looked straight into his face, and spoke slowly. "We don't have time for this."

"You just said we have to do the things that are important," he chirped. Now I was sure he was just out to drive me crazy.

Using that unique tone of voice usually restricted to third-grade teachers who are about to lose their minds, I said, "Daniel, get off the monkey bars and get back to work."

His smile only got bigger. "Karen, get on the monkey bars and start to play. Just for a while. Come on. It's fun."

My choices were to get angry and hope he would do things my way, or to give up. I decided to let my discomfort pass. Releasing my aggravation with a deep sigh, I grasped the monkey bars and pulled myself up. I remembered this . . . feeling ten feet tall, up above everyone else, looking down on the tops of the other kids' heads. Hooking my legs around the bars, I allowed myself to fall backward. My body turned upside down, and I was surprised to hear myself laugh. For a few happy moments, I swung back and forth, watching the other kids play.

"You have a right to play, too." Daniel's face grew closer and farther, closer and farther away as I swung back and forth. He was standing in the sand, looking concerned. I untangled my feet, flipped over, and stood next to him. His ability to know what I was thinking was unnerving.

"How do you do that? How do you know what's going on in my mind?"

"Let's go swing." The king of the non sequitur settled himself into a swing, pumped his legs, and set a course for the sky.

"Okay, okay," I muttered. Somehow, I was not really displeased. After all, what could the harm be in taking some time to play in the park? I laughed out loud as I flew high in the air. Why not? After what I had been through today, why not?

◖ EIGHT ◗

I looked out across the fields surrounding the swings as I used my legs to push me higher. Daniel was right beside me, wearing a grin almost too big for his face.

"See, this is really fun!" he called out, his body passing by on its way backward as I went forward. I had to admit, it was fun. Actually, it was great!

I thought about how long it had been since I had been on the swings. In my final spring at grade school, I went outside late one afternoon and sat on the swings. I was feeling strangely sad. All year, I had looked forward to escaping elementary school. Suddenly, it was time to leave and all I felt was an empty ache inside. I cried for everything I was leaving behind. Somehow, what was coming didn't make up for what was to be lost.

When the coming summer ended, I wouldn't be entering the same glass doors and finding my way to a new classroom. This building would no longer be the comfortable place I had come to rely on. I would no longer see the faces I had depended on to keep me safe. I wouldn't be allowed to be the same person I had been. I wasn't going to be able to cry like this, I decided. I couldn't go to the swings anymore. Somehow, I would have to know everything, and not ask stupid questions. If I got scared, I would have to pretend I was strong.

I thought about it all and grudgingly left it behind in one intense, private ceremony of loss. Once I heard somebody say that everything in life is a trade-off. That day I traded my child-hood for my adolescence, and once done, it seemed gone for-ever. Lost in my thoughts, I had not noticed that Daniel had stopped swinging.

"What's the matter?"

"Look," he said, so quietly I wasn't certain I had heard him correctly. I slowed down and asked him again, only to hear the same one-word answer.

"Look at what? I don't see anything." My body now at a full stop, my gaze was fixed in the same direction as his. Glanc-ing over at him, I found he had started across the park. Even as I was running after this mysterious child, I considered how important he had become in such a short time. Nothing had been the same since I first saw him.

The last thing I could consider normal was sitting on a plane on my way to Seattle. Since then, I had been out to space and down to Boise and away to see God. At least that's where I thought we were going. Suddenly, I realized Daniel had never said we were going to see God.

We walked together for what seemed like an hour. We passed a steep, weedy hill, the ultimate challenge to childhood courage. I remembered gathering up a big piece of cardboard, sitting on it, and shoving off. The paper sled would careen down the hill, bucking screaming children from its back like some primitive beast. Great glory came to anyone who could stay on board.

Daniel and I continued to walk silently, crossing the river that wound all the way through the city. I had spent wonderful hours sloshing along in such a river, catching pollywogs and setting them free again. The slick, deep green mud at the bottom would squish between my toes, and my mind would create wild stories of adventure and heroism. I was so alive.

Maybe those precious gifts of childhood were simply the

result of freedom from responsibility. A child has time to do whatever he wants to do. He has no worries; adults do everything for him. Once childhood is gone, it's gone. You have work and responsibilities, and the next generation gets to play. That's the way it is supposed to be.

Walking under the graceful arms of the oak trees that lined the street, I felt a sensation in my chest. A deep sadness challenged the conventional logic that had made perfect sense a moment ago. I found myself feeling something I hadn't allowed for a long time. Suddenly all of that logic was only a comfortable explanation for what really was a tragic loss.

A child's exquisite ability to be alive, to be in rhythm with himself, was not due to having more time. He just hadn't closed himself off and shut down his capacity to respond to the gifts of the moment. He was still able to see everything and feel everything. He wasn't carrying around a list of instructions about how to control it all.

I used to be like that! Bit by bit, my openness and connection with everything got replaced by heaviness and fear. The adult became a container for concerns about an artificial life. Who thinks what of me? What will I do if this happens? How am I going to pay my bills? How can I get what I want? The child who knew how to be alive—where did she go? Had I managed to kill her off?

It's not time that goes away; it's our very essence that gets destroyed. Focused on what we have to do, we never even notice the absence of that purest part of ourselves. And without it, life becomes only an obstacle course, an endless series of problems to be solved.

I looked carefully at the boy beside me. He smiled before saying softly, "That's it, Karen. That's it."

ဢ NINE ဢ

No longer surprised at his ability to read my mind, I accepted the slip of his hand into mine and responded with the passion I was feeling. "Daniel . . . what happens to us? I want to be the way I used to be. I want to feel the way I used to feel."

"You just get mixed up," he replied. "Every time you come here, it takes a long time just to figure out that you're all mixed up. Then you get started figuring it out, and you usually don't have enough time to finish it. So you just have to try to remember all over again. I don't know why it works like that, but it does."

He conveyed this information in a completely matter-of-fact way. He seemed oddly cheerful about it. I felt like I had just listened to a child's review of a movie. It almost makes sense, but you really can't put the pieces together.

"I'm afraid I don't understand."

"Of course you don't understand!" he said emphatically. "How can you understand something if you can't remember? That's why it's so hard. You have to know to look for something even though you don't remember it at all."

I tried to make sense of his words. "Daniel, I don't have any idea what you're talking about." I didn't feel impatient with him, only anxious to have information that clearly was going to be very important to me. "Can you back up and explain what you're saying?"

He took in a breath and started again, "You don't remember that you don't remember until you know you have something you have to remember. Then you start to remember and it gets better, but usually not better enough before you forget again."

He smiled, pleased at his apparent accomplishment. I was stumped. Clearly, he was trying to tell me something I needed to know, but the harder he tried, the more it sounded like gibberish. I did my best to glean something from his sentences. "I need to remember something?"

"How do you know that you know something?"

"Well, it comes easily to mind. You don't have to struggle with it. You're confident about it."

He looked at me for a moment and then asked, "Suppose something was true in your head, but wasn't true anywhere else . . . how would you know?"

"Evidence." That was easy. Everyone knew that empirical evidence was the hallmark of truth. I looked over at him.

He was not satisfied with my simple answer. "Suppose what you call evidence was only what you saw, because it was the only thing you knew to look for. And there was a lot of other stuff you never even noticed."

I said softly, "Well, I guess you'd end up with only part of the truth . . . the part you knew to look for." Daniel's eyes met mine, and I suddenly felt like Christopher Columbus was about to tell me the world wasn't flat anymore.

"Right!" he said enthusiastically. "What if the stuff you didn't even know to look for was way bigger than the stuff you knew?" He smiled up at me, an expression I was beginning to regard with a peculiar anxiety.

"It would have to catch up with you eventually. . . ." My words trailed off as my stomach sent up a warning that the world was about to shift sideways.

"Yep . . . well, it's caught up," he said, walking off in a new direction. "Come on, there's something I want you to see."

"Wait a minute. Wait!" I stumbled after him. "I don't want any more confusion than I already have. Daniel, I don't want to see anything. Unless . . . are we going to meet God now? Are you finally going to take me there?"

Starting in mid-topic, he replied, "I always thought it would be a good idea to just show somebody what it's all about. They just keep sending teacher after teacher to Earth and what happens? Usually, the people find a way to get rid of the teacher. Look what happened to Jesus!"

He stopped speaking, and I struggled to find a way to understand what he had just said. "Daniel, are you talking about God . . . the angels . . . is God about to reveal Himself?"

Daniel began to laugh again. His amusement about my questions was getting to be insulting. I was doing the best I could do. My God . . . what a day! How did he expect me to respond? But I had to admit that whenever he giggled everything seemed manageable again.

The little boy threw up his arms and said, "Karen, you just have to know about God, don't you?" He watched my confusion for a second and continued. "See, that's what keeps getting all the people in such trouble . . . they have to know about God, but they don't really know, and so they keep making things up. I told everybody we should just let one person see everything; then it wouldn't be so hard to get their attention."

"See everything?"

His voice sounded a little sad. "Well, everybody's so lost, you can't find anything, especially yourselves! When somebody tries to help you, you never listen."

Not hesitating long enough to allow me to catch up, Daniel continued to talk. "Every time a teacher is sent, all he can do is talk a lot. But people only hear what they have already learned, and they never understand what he says. They get so happy when they can take something really big and get it all squashed down into something really little. But once it's squashed, it's squashed, know what I mean?"

He looked up at me with his bright, open face and I gave his question my best shot. "Daniel, are you saying somebody out there keeps sending teachers to Earth so that people can understand God, but nobody ever comprehends what they say?"

He looked as though he would like to reward my effort, but then replied, "Sort of . . . kind of . . . well, that's not exactly right . . . but . . ."

I took in another deep breath. "Tell me again."

"Well, it's more like the truth keeps showing up, but nobody wants to listen."

I remained confused. "Isn't that the same thing?"

"Sort of . . . kind of," he began.

I finished for him, "Not exactly."

His eyes searched mine. "See, people always want to know what reality is. What's the truth? What they never get is that there are bunches of truths and realities all at the same time. We try to tell them, but they never like it! They always say, 'Yes, but what is really true?' It depends on how you know how to look and what kind of a heart you have."

"That's not so hard to understand, Daniel," I said with relief. "Everybody knows that people see things differently."

"They might know about people's different opinions about stuff, but they sure don't know about how people live in different worlds."

My heart sank. "What?"

His attitude was matter-of-fact. "People . . . they live in different worlds . . . you know, depending on what kind of heart and way of seeing they have. A really long time ago, people could see and know everything, but they forgot. Want to know why?"

"Of course I want to know why," I cried. "Daniel, I haven't come all this way to bail out now! What happened? Why did they forget?"

"You'll see how it is," was all he said.

ೞ TEN ೞ

I was getting used to this business of instantly being somewhere else. It had possibilities; maybe I could learn to think myself wherever I wanted to go and forget airplanes all together. Perhaps I could learn how to get myself to the office without a car.

"Where are we?" I asked quietly, looking out over a lovely green valley.

He smiled. "We're not in Boise. But it really doesn't matter where we are. People do the same thing all over Earth. They think they are different from each other . . . you know, those lines they draw on the maps . . . they treat them like they're real. What a silly idea to think you can divide the Earth up and pretend everybody's different, by sitting somewhere and drawing lines on a piece of paper . . . don't you think that's a funny thing to do?"

I didn't know what to say. It had never really occurred to me that dividing ourselves into different nations was a ridiculous thing to do. But I remembered reading a quote from Chief Joseph of the Nez Perce people. He said, "We are all alike, brothers of the one father and one mother, with one sky above us and one government for all. When we live this, then the great spirit chief who rules above will smile upon this land and send rain to wash out the bloody spots from the face of the Earth that were made by brothers' hands."

I felt ashamed of myself. I had read those beautiful words

and put them aside as romantic Indian lore. I knew there was much Native American wisdom that I had ignored as leftovers from history. I had done the same with ideals about the universal brotherhood of man. They are glorious concepts that never work. Most of us can't even get along with our auto mechanic, let alone somebody from the other side of the world.

We all get misty-eyed around Christmas time, but the feeling vaporizes as quickly as the illusion that we really had enough money to pay for all the things we were seduced into buying. January depression . . . bills and that sinking realization that worldwide peace and harmony is a great dream; too bad it doesn't work out that way. What was this child trying to tell me?

"So what happened, Daniel? You started to tell me about how people used to be able to see everything and know everything. I just want to say, that's contrary to what we're taught. I mean, humans have developed from the animals, and we are getting better and better at managing ourselves and the world. We're more intelligent, not less."

"Is it intelligent to murder each other and destroy your home?" he asked softly. I was surprised to see his eyes fill with tears. "While you are busy counting how many more machines you can build, your people are suffering all over the planet. Do you want to know why?"

"Yes, yes, tell me why!" Did he really have an answer to such an enormous question?

"Well, you guys live in the mud and you make more of it every day. That's what's really sad. I think that if we could just get you to stop doing that kind of stuff, everything would . . ."

"Wait, wait . . . hold it!" The engine was rolling down the tracks without the rest of the train. What was he talking about? I found myself cracking my knuckles one at a time, something

I only do under stress. Flying all over the place without a co-herent companion qualifies as stress. Extreme stress.

Then Daniel suddenly blurted out, "Whoops, I forgot."

I stared at him and continued to abuse my fingers.

He shrugged and said, "I forgot, you don't remember about density."

I found my voice. "Density . . . to me, that word means something thick."

"That's a good way to understand it," he replied brightly. "See, everything is made of energy and it's all moving really quick. You know that from school, right?"

"Well, that's elementary physics, yes."

He was filled with enthusiasm, "Okay . . . if something moves really fast without being blocked and its atoms are really far apart, then what?"

"Well, it's lighter, more transparent, less in the way." I liked having the answers for a change.

His little face looked at me with an odd intensity. "Karen, do you mean you could see through it more easily . . . see what might be beyond it?"

"I suppose so. That would be one of the characteristics."

He nodded, apparently happy that I could follow what he was saying. "So, what was meant to be light and translucent got all messed up and slowed down and got very thick and ran into itself and everything else. Like when the power goes off . . . it makes that sound . . . RRRrrrUUmmmmm . . . you know, slow. That's what I meant when I said you were all living in the mud."

I felt I had suddenly taken a wrong turn and was about to fall off the trail. "Are you telling me that the energy of Earth itself used to be different?"

He gazed up for a second and said, "Kind of . . . sort of . . ."

I knew my part. "Not exactly."

"Earth's energy itself would be fine if all the people who lived on Earth didn't build up density." His eyes took in the natural scene around us. "It's not Earth that's the problem . . . it's the choices people keep making."

I wasn't sure I really wanted to ask for clarification.

But he was intent on increasing my understanding and quickly went on, "Before you built up density, your energy was moving really fast, and Earth's energy was moving really fast, too. You were able to work together. But by making the choices you make over and over again, it all gets thick and heavy and you lose all of your abilities. Next thing you know, the only thing you consider is the stuff you can find with your body senses . . . you know, what you can see and taste and smell and hear . . . just the obvious. Then you have to do everything at a thick level. You just get more and more angry and upset, and hurt each other and Earth."

I was still confused. "I guess I don't understand what density has to do with how we treat each other."

He thought for a moment and continued, "Well, when everything slows way down, that makes it look like there's such a thing as something solid. If something's solid, then it's separate from the next thing that's solid. People start to see things in a really limited way. I mean, if everything's solid and separate, then you have to make sure you compete with the other people to get what you need . . . because, if it's all unconnected, you can't just receive what you need.

"People start to fight for survival with their hands and weapons. Things have to be either won or lost. Stuff you need has to be pulled out of the earth with a lot of pain. Other people turn into objects. Things to be moved around and used by one another. It's really awfully sad . . ." he said, walking off through some wildflowers.

Following him, I found myself wanting to argue, but curiously, I didn't have much enthusiasm for it. "Daniel, competition is necessary. That's how we get what we need . . ." I paused, unable to continue with something that didn't seem correct anymore. "Tell me another way."

His little face lit up at my willingness to learn. "Well, somebody who is full of density can only make something that matches that. If he can only use his senses because all the rest of his abilities are clogged up, he struggles really hard and ends up with only what he can make out of the most obvious stuff. Maybe that wouldn't be so sad, except that he doesn't even know he's doing that! He thinks reality exists outside of himself and that he's just supposed to recognize it. But really, he creates his own world. He can use density to create, or he can do it with truth.

"There's so much more that you could use when you make your reality. Instead, people limit themselves and make systems to decide what things can be real and what can't. But they're only using what they know to include and exclude, not really determining what's imaginary and what's true. Excluding something only makes it nonexistent for the person who did the excluding. It doesn't really affect its existence in reality.

"Isn't this the most beautiful thing?" He had stopped and crouched down over a tiny plant. I peered over his shoulder.

"What is it?" My voice conveyed a desire to be polite.

"See, Karen?" he said sadly. "That's what I mean. Your mind immediately wants to put a name on it, take it apart, put it in its place as something dangerous or something safe to ignore. But look at it closely."

I had gotten somewhat used to the fact that I was going to have to do things that didn't make sense to me if I was going to continue being in the company of this little guy. I knelt down beside him and reached out my finger to carefully touch the plant.

"What do you see?" he asked quietly.

I didn't know what he wanted me to say. "I see an inter-esting plant that I would like to look up in one of my gardening books." I was proud of my botanical library. By using the in-formation contained within those books, I had learned to grow practically anything.

Sounding exasperated, he said, "You see, your mind wants to pull you far away from where you really are. Don't let that happen, Karen. What do you see?"

I stared uncomfortably at the little growing thing. It ap-peared to be some kind of fern . . . no, he said not to name it. "Well, it's a bright green plant of some sort." There. I hoped I had done something right.

"What else?"

I gave it another try, "It seems to be doing quite well . . . clearly, it is well suited to its location." What did he want from me?

"What else? What else can you see, Karen?" The voice was very, very faint and the world had gone completely green.

✂ ELEVEN ✂

Jumping to my feet, I expected to pull clear of the all-encompassing color. Instead, I found myself surrounded by spectacular beauty. Enormous, vibrant trees swayed around me, like giant drifts of seaweed caught on a gentle current. Emerald green, they were unlike anything I had ever seen before.

"Daniel," I whispered as I slowly turned around. "Where are we?"

The little voice seemed to bypass my ears; I simply heard him clearly in my mind. "What do you see? Tell me what you see, Karen."

For the moment unconcerned that the boy didn't seem anywhere nearby, I answered quietly, "I'm in some kind of forest. Daniel, there are the most incredibly beautiful trees here!"

I heard him repeat, "Tell me what you see."

My heart was full of appreciation for the vision before me. Not wanting to miss any of it, I almost forgot to answer him. "They're moving somehow, opening and closing what appear to be giant fans. I didn't know trees like this existed. Daniel, are we in the rain forest?"

"What do you see?"

I allowed my feet to take a few steps forward and took in a wider view before I responded, "Astounding beauty! These trees are as graceful as ballet dancers, moving back and forth together as if music must be playing somewhere." I paused to watch them and suddenly realized what they were doing. "They're reaching for the sunshine! Daniel, they're stretching upward, spreading out their leaves to reach for the light."

I knew he wanted me to continue. "I can see the sun coming down inside them! Now they have become transparent somehow. I can see sparkling bits of light moving down through them. It's just pouring into them and flowing around inside. God, it's breathtaking. Everything is moving, the light, the trees and it smells so good, so green, so alive!"

I was transfixed by the fullness of it all. This place was a realm of magic and movement, the air so sweet. Mesmerized, I wondered about spending a lifetime in a place like this, just watching the sunlight finding its way into the trees. In the midst of this perfection, I felt incredible peace inside. How could I preserve this feeling? I had no idea where I was or how I had gotten here, but perhaps I could persuade Daniel to let me stay for a while.

Suddenly my body went rapidly backward, and I caught my breath in time to see the tiny green thing under my nose. I was back in the field, crouched on my knees. Beside me was the familiar laughter.

"Isn't it good to see?" the boy asked, his arms outstretched to call attention to his point.

"What . . . what was that?" I gasped, my heart trying to beat a path out of my chest. "Where was I?"

"Inside the fern, silly!" he replied with a grin. "Where did you think you were?" Not waiting for my stunned expression to fade, he went off through the field in search of other treasures.

"Wait!" I scrambled after him, being especially careful not to step on that little fern. "Wait . . . Daniel, just a minute. You can't just tell me I've been inside a plant and then walk off . . . wait! How did you do that?"

"Helped you drop your density . . . that's all," he said happily. "Like I keep telling you, the only reason you don't have all your abilities is 'cause you keep building up mud." He skipped a few steps, turned himself all the way around, and then, seeing my new desire to learn burning within me, stopped.

"Look around. What do you see?" He sounded excited, and I did as I was told.

"Well, I see lots of flowers and trees, some grass, a few boulders, and some birds."

"Look again," he commanded. "This time, pay attention to the fact that they're all the same thing."

"I don't understand."

"Just go ahead," he said, encouraging me. "See what you can see."

Gazing out over the field, I tried to consider how trees and boulders and birds could possibly be the same thing. I looked around more carefully. There was something about this place, a pulsing quality, like the soft breath of a sleeping kitten.

Staring at a large, speckled rock, I tried to see what was strange. It seemed very happy. "Happy" was the perfect word, yet it seemed ridiculous. How could a rock be happy? But then, everything I was seeing looked happy. Actually, it all looked joyful.

"Just keep looking, Karen. You'll see."

The little boy at my side sounded so confident and encouraging. As I fixed my attention on the rock, determined to experience whatever Daniel was talking about, it changed dramatically. For a fraction of a second, I could see inside it. Like an incandescent newspaper photograph, the rock was made up of tiny, sparkling particles of light vibrating in space.

"Daniel!" I said excitedly. "I could see inside that rock! I could see light inside that rock."

"Try looking at that bush," he said.

My mind rapidly assessed the object in front of me. "Okay, it's some kind of shrubby pine, doing quite well, would do better with more water."

Daniel chastised me gently. "You need to just look, Karen. Don't name it or judge it, just see what it is."

It suddenly occurred to me that I might be able to see energy moving in the pine, too. As soon as I allowed for the possibility, the little bush revealed itself. Scarcely willing to take in a breath, I desperately wanted to continue to see particles of light glittering before my eyes.

"That's it. I knew you could do it!"

This was incredible. Of course, I knew about atoms and electrons and molecules. I had known intellectually that everything was made up of these tiny, moving particles of energy. But to see it! How could a human being see these things without a machine?

Daniel looked up at me. "How do you think anyone ever figured out they needed to invent a machine that could see the energy?"

"Well, they just progressed along with the scientific method until they realized a machine was needed, and then they built one." Although what I had said was certainly logical, I knew inside that it was wrong.

We're all taught that science is the ultimate example of man's ability to reason. The scientific method is the only route to true knowledge. I remembered my statistics professor sarcastically comparing research based on mathematical computations with research based on interviewing people. I had learned then that what people perceived was never reliable; but a carefully constructed experiment—now that was valuable.

Daniel interrupted my ruminations. "Actually, they already knew what they built the machine to find out. They just built the machine because they forgot exactly how to see it without one." His words were matter-of-fact, but shocking.

"What do you mean, they already knew?" I cried. "How could they know? That's what science is all about . . . venturing into the unknown."

"Well, science is like that, but it's the long way to go about it," he said, as if that should have been perfectly obvious. "Besides, even science doesn't always work that way. Think about what happens sometimes. A whole way of understanding something, even one that came straight out of science, gets thrown out and a new thing turns out to be more true! It isn't just collecting facts and building on them, is it?"

Well, he had a point. "You mean like Einstein changing the way we think about energy and matter?"

"Yep," he replied with a grin. "Now, didn't all the scientists up to then think they were doing a great job? And they were doing wonderfully at collecting facts, but the truth was bigger than the facts. And, what was different about Einstein?"

The reality of what he was saying acted like a depth charge in my stomach. "He was willing to look past what everyone else was seeing?"

"Right!" The little boy beamed. "He was willing to look inside to what he knew was true."

"He knew about relativity all along? He didn't discover it by objective research?" Albert Einstein was an icon, our best example of the intellectual mind, and it turned out he wasn't scientific at all!

"Yep," he said with a nod. "All the fact collecting and machines, it's just what people have to do because they've forgotten what they already know. If they would include themselves in their studies, they would know what they forgot a lot faster. But your whole scientific method is based on removing the person who already knows what he wants to know!"

The little pine still had spaces in it. I slowly shifted my attention to a nearby tree. It was spacious too. "Daniel, I think I've got it down. I can see the spaces in the pine, the boulder, and the tree!" I was so proud of myself.

"Okay, now look at yourself," he said. Suddenly, I was frightened. I didn't really want to see spaces in myself. I liked being a solid human being. The idea of being able to watch my own particulate matter roam around was unsettling, to say the least.

"It's all right, Karen. You can do it. You're only giving up an idea of what you are. Nothing will change except your awareness of what is real."

What did that mean? Of course I was real . . . but maybe I was real in a different way from what I had thought. After all, I had gotten out of an airplane in midflight without dying, and I had just journeyed to the inside of a fern. I looked down. My legs, arms, stomach, and chest were all there, and they were all different. I was full of moving dots of energy, just like the boulder, the tree and the bush!

But there was something alarming about what I saw. "Daniel, look at me! I'm so empty. There's so much empty space in here! Is this okay? Is this the way I'm supposed to look?"

"Oh, Karen, don't you see?" he exclaimed. "Spinning atoms whirling in space is what you see as matter. But your body is only one percent matter and ninety-nine percent empty space. Who do you suppose lives in all that empty space?"

"Me?" I said lamely, hardly able to comprehend what he was saying.

"Of course it's you, silly! You organize the matter and tell it how to spin. The intelligence that creates your body lives in the darkness between the atoms. Don't look at yourself as the one percent, when you're really so much bigger than that!"

"That's what you were trying to tell me about density . . ."

I suddenly lost track of the thought that had seemed crystal clear a second ago.

Daniel smiled softly and said, "See, if you think you're just a thick, machinelike thing, then you make a world that complements that. And if you see that you are a being of energy, you create a corresponding reality. It's your choice."

Afraid to sound crazy, I whispered my question. "Are you telling me it's all what we create?"

"Uh-huh. And most of what you produce is so dense, it takes the density of the physical body to meet it and move it around. What you call 'reality' is filled with density, something so thick you can actually encounter it by just using your physical senses."

My mind refused to work. Daniel watched me struggle and then abruptly said, "Here, come over to this tree." Taking my hand, he carefully placed my palm against the smooth bark of a red maple. "See, when your hand is hard and dense, then the tree is, too." He lifted my hand away from the tree. "Now, see your hand the way it really is . . . just like you saw your body a moment ago."

I tried to focus on what I had learned. Closing my eyes, I practiced the idea that my body was not really the solid thing it appeared to be. I was spacious, not thick. I was energy in the form of a physical body. My eyes flew open as my hand suddenly gave way to sparkling particles.

"Now, put your hand back on the tree."

I followed his direction and found the tree was no longer solid either. When I touched it, I could stay on its surface, or move my hand right through it!

"Now, is the tree real?"

I was overwhelmed by my magical experience. "Of course the tree is real, but not the way we've always seen it!"

"For what you just did, you have to have intent."

"Intent?" I found myself patting the tree, which was solid again.

"If you want something to happen on an energy level, you need to focus your awareness. If you decide that's what you truly want, that is what will be."

Some part of me was appalled. "Daniel, how could that be? Isn't that just wishful thinking? Pretending? Denying reality?"

"Did you put your hand through that tree with a wish?"

"Well, no." I was utterly confused. I couldn't argue with my experience. I had just put my hand straight through an object that had always seemed solid.

"Well, how did you do it?" he prompted.

My mind was in a terrific battle with itself, but I decided to try simply repeating what Daniel had taught me. "I changed the way I saw myself, and by doing so I was able to see the tree."

He would not let me off the hook so easily. "Is there a difference between that and wishful thinking?"

I replied uneasily, "Well, one has to do with sitting around wishing things were different and the other with actually doing something different."

Then my mind sent up another defense. "But what about reality, Daniel? We all have to deal with certain things."

"Why?" he answered innocently.

I could feel the voices of every parent I had ever known speaking within me. "Because they're there, that's all. Certain things exist, and we have to deal with them."

"Why?" he repeated.

"Daniel! Because they are there."

"Why are things there?" He looked at me blankly, and I wrestled with my frustration. What did he want me to say— "No, they aren't there"?

"Daniel, they are there because they are there."

"Like a body which absolutely must have an airplane to fly?

Like trees and bushes and boulders are hard and unmoving?" He stopped, and I somehow felt his compassionate support while I allowed his words to blow me apart.

My last vestige of security gave way, accompanied by the sensation of a drop in blood pressure. "Daniel," I said weakly, "how can we ever know what is true?"

"Well," he began, looking up into the sky, "the truth is very simple and the confusion is very complicated. That's one way. See, it's what I've been trying to tell you. You just need to remember who you really are."

"Where do I even begin?" How could I dismantle the concepts that provided the framework for my mind?

"Well, you have to always remember something important." He waited for me to ask what.

I could not keep quiet for long. "What? What should I remember?"

"That nothing, absolutely nothing, is as it appears to be . . . even when you are certain." He smiled and added, "Maybe I should say especially when you are certain."

"But what do I do differently?"

"You can start by making new choices. Everything you do either increases or decreases your density. Look at the food you eat; is it dead or full of chemicals? Just like the fern you saw, your body wants to take in beautiful, life-giving energy. Look at where you spend time. Are these places full of concrete and noise? Everything is made of energy . . . find the places that are still alive."

He watched my uncertainty begin to lift and went on with renewed enthusiasm. "Look at who you spend time with. Are those people filled with anger and heaviness? Do you feel burdened after you've been around them? Look at how you live. What things can you let go of? Can you allow yourself to stop being busy and only do what's really important?"

I considered what he had told me and then said soberly, "All those rules . . . I don't want to live like a nun, Daniel."

"Well, you know everything's free will! And they're not rules, just suggestions. See, that's how teaching gets distorted! Like your Ten Commandments, they were never meant as commandments, just suggestions about how you can set down density."

"Daniel . . ." I found myself laughing. "The Ten Suggestions?"

He replied with a nod. "Just some good ideas about staying free of density. And there's nobody out there to punish you if you don't follow them. The thing is, you are the one who suffers if you make a choice to pick up more density! You might want to think about whether what you have is really what you want. When it's three o'clock in the morning, that ache you sometimes feel in your chest . . . could it be that there really aren't enough distractions in the world to relieve that pain?"

How did he know about my three A.M. blues? When it was dark and silent, sometimes I wondered if what I had was really all there was to life. I mean, you spend a lot of time trying to be successful. It seems like the most important thing you can do for yourself and your family. But after you have the nice house and the great stuff . . . well, there was a certain emptiness. When it came to your last few breaths, would it matter what kind of car was parked in the driveway?

I didn't bother to deny these feelings. "What's density got to do with that ache, Daniel?"

"It keeps you separate . . . that's the main thing. It makes you forget how everything is connected. That ache is about suffering from an awful loneliness." He watched me carefully. "Somewhere inside, you know you've been cut off from something important. Once you are cut off, you kind of close up and start to get thick . . . then you get scared."

I didn't want that to be true of me. I tried to find a way to make it personally inapplicable. "But I have a great relationship. We share everything. We're very close . . ." Despite my effort, I already knew that was not what he meant.

"That's part of the confusion! When you're cut off from all the connectedness, you have to attach yourself to other people. You try to substitute them for what you really need. Imagine being by a beautiful, clear lake that offered all the water you could ever need. But you forgot it was there and you started to die of thirst. If somebody came by with even a thimbleful of water, you'd think he was the most important person in the world. You would be desperate to make sure he was always right there. You'd start figuring out ways to keep him around. That doesn't have much to do with love . . . not really." With that, he started walking again.

"Well, what are we supposed to connect with?" I was feeling my frustration return. Suddenly, I thought I had the answer! "That's why we need to find God!"

I was dumbfounded when Daniel looked over at me, apparently exasperated. "That's exactly how you all get lost! How do we get you to give up looking into the sky for the answers? Your Earth gods make it so hard!"

I stopped in my tracks and Daniel innocently asked, "Why'd you stop? Come on, I want you to see."

"Wait a minute," I choked. "Did you say something about Earth gods . . . what does that mean? You said, 'gods,' plural . . . and Earth . . . isn't God in charge of it all? What do you mean, the Earth gods?"

"Well, just look."

I really didn't like that phrase. Every time Daniel said those words, something difficult was about to happen. Nevertheless, I looked out past his pointed finger and caught my breath.

⦗ TWELVE ⦘

We were well beyond the Earth, but I could see the vibrant blue sphere turning in the blackness, beautiful as ever. But now there were four enormous male figures surrounding it. Jostling for territory, each appeared several times larger than the Earth.

Astounded, I managed to whisper, "What are those?"

"Those are the Earth gods, all four of them. You know, Yahweh, Jehovah, the evil one, and the nameless, faceless one."

"Yahweh and Jehovah. That's God in the Bible . . . the evil one, that's what some people call Satan." I trailed off, terrified to hear his answer.

"And the nameless, faceless one is what lots of other religions think of as God. Pretty scary things to create, don't you think? That's density for you. It makes ugly stuff."

"What's that coming out from the Earth?" I managed to choke out my question, afraid the God of my childhood would turn and dismiss my existence with a thought.

"That's all the energy of the human beings going up to feed the Earth gods," he said sadly. "They can't even exist unless you continue to give up your own power. The people of Earth created them and keep them going every time they look outside themselves for instructions and help."

I allowed this astounding information to sink in, then something occured to me. "Wait a minute, Daniel. Aren't Yahweh and Jehovah the same thing? Why are there two of them?"

"No." he answered. "They aren't the same at all. Yahweh was first. He was created out of the misunderstandings about the old part of your Bible. Jehovah was born of the confusion about the new part of the Bible."

"Oh." I struggled for a moment. "Well, what about Allah? A lot of people on Earth worship Him."

"The names aren't important," he answered. "What matters is the kind of energy humans send up to create the different Earth gods. Some of the people who worship Allah are really giving energy to Yahweh, and some are feeding Jehovah. It depends on whether they're confused traditionalists or mixed-up fundamentalists."

His little arms were crossed over his chest, and he looked intensely serious. We stood together and watched the steady streams of energy flowing upward from Earth. The Earth gods fought to catch the resources being sent. At the moment, it appeared that Jehovah was winning, but the evil one seemed almost as strong.

"What's that foggy-looking thing out to the side?" I asked, watching an amorphous figure drift just beyond the range of the four competitors.

"Oh, that's the new one," he replied, a hint of sarcasm in his voice. "People have created another Earth god for themselves. They call it 'the light.' It's just the most recent invention of something outside they can look to."

Seeing my confusion, he added, "Some people started to realize that God must be different from what they had been taught. They turned away from the old ideas, but they just ended up making another Earth god. The other ones think it's funny, you know, humans believing they can get away from them. The new god just helps keep people from understanding the truth."

"Daniel, is there any hope for us?" I said desperately. "I

thought the light was a positive thing, something apart from religious institutions. What's wrong with that?"

"It could have been good. But 'the light' is still outside the person, and still more powerful, and still requires that a person turn to it for help."

Suddenly, Daniel threw out his arms. "Let them go," he shouted. "Just leave them alone. Leave those people alone!"

Daniel was yelling at God, and I had nowhere to hide. There was nowhere to go and nothing to do but wait for the inevitable repercussions.

What happens if God decides to wipe you out? But which god? There were almost five of them out here. There was only supposed to be one God! And I could see the beautiful, shimmering energy being sapped from the Earth by these five false gods.

None of them was paying the slightest bit of attention to Daniel's outburst. "Daniel, why aren't they responding to you?"

"Because they know perfectly well that Earth is a planet of free will," he said angrily. "They don't have anything to worry about as long as people continue to believe in them. You know, if people would just stop, those guys would be gone instantly."

"How did they get started? Where did they come from in the first place?"

"Power and confusion . . . simple as that. When people started to get confused, other people started taking advantage of that confusion. Those people had lost track of who they really are, too, but no one knew that."

I looked at him blankly. "Who are you talking about?"

"Your religious leaders. I call them keepers of the buildings. They do a good job of taking care of pretty churches and temples and an awful job of reminding people about who they really are."

It was beginning to occur to me that our religious leaders

might not know any more than we did about the reality of these Earth gods. I dared to ask, "Daniel, do they know the answer? Do they know who we really are?"

"Most of them have forgotten completely." Watching my reaction, he added, "But the thing is, nobody knows that. Mostly, people think ministers and priests have some special connection to God. But secretly, most of the keepers know they don't have any connection. They can't admit it, or they'd lose their position and their power."

I was about to ask him if there was anybody on Earth who knew the answers, when he continued. "There are people who do know more, but a lot of them decide not to tell 'cause people wouldn't need them anymore."

Suddenly, we were in a room. It seemed like a long time ago. I could see several robed figures sitting in a circle. They looked like priests of some kind. It was cold here; the continuous rain fed dusky mold that covered the stone floor.

"They can't hear you or see you," Daniel said softly. Somehow, I could perceive more than the words being spoken.

"The people must never have this." Their quiet words barely disturbed the air. Meeting in daylight, the men held no fear of being seen. There was no need for emphasis; each man in the circle felt the message hit hard in his solar plexus.

"It would mean the end of everything." Like the wind touching weeds in a field, their heads nodded silently in agreement. Under the subtle glow of gemstones and the flicker of gold, their hearts were cold. Their people were terrified, and that was good.

"How can we contain this?" one said uneasily, his robe registering a shift in rigid posture. "It almost seems destined to become known." He bowed his dark head, unwilling to meet the judgmental eyes, frightened that the others might think him disloyal.

"We will do what is necessary. We must give them a story they can accept and hide the rest. No one would dare question us." The man looked at the others, hoping to find in them the courage he only pretended to hold.

"How long . . . ?" The white hands glistened with moisture from fear. Twisting, the fingers ground against each other with anxiety. "How long will we have?" The voice trembled and the man shook.

"Perhaps forever," a stronger note sounded. "It will all be ours. After all, who among them will ever ask?"

"Daniel . . . Daniel," I whispered, afraid of being seen.

He spoke at full volume. "Don't worry; remember they can't hear you or see you."

"Who are these people?" I asked. "What are they trying to hide?"

"Just what is most important in the whole world . . . who you really are. It doesn't matter who they are. There have been people like this all along, all over your world, in all the different religions. Looking for spiritual guidance can be a dangerous thing. A teacher should only help you to remember who you are. If he's telling you what to do and how to think, he's only a keeper."

"How can we ever figure out what's true?" My head was pounding. This was too much for me to sort out by myself. Even though I hadn't figured out the answers to life's mysteries, I always thought it was because I hadn't devoted enough time to the classics, philosophy, Hebrew, something. Everybody has a Bible, or a Talmud or a Koran, but few people read them. You decide someday you will, and then you'll understand the important things. I always thought it was a matter of studying the right things. Wasn't that what religious leaders were supposed to be doing?

"Daniel . . . if what we thought was God isn't really God, what is it?"

"A really dangerous distraction," he replied quietly. "As long as people stay focused on that, they'll never remember."

My mind went into overdrive. "Daniel, are you telling me all of our great teachers have been mixed up? You mean, we all learned garbled messages about what God is, and what we are?"

He didn't flinch. "Yep."

His answer was so simple and so complete, I was stopped for a moment. The whole thing was mind-boggling. Getting off an airplane in midflight was easy compared to entertaining the idea that what I had always thought was God was only something birthed into reality by the misguided actions of man. Our own fear and confusion had jelled into a being that terrified us. We gave Him life, then fell to our knees and begged for His forgiveness!

"Daniel, what you've told me is blasphemy!" I felt a rush of fear, familiar and painful. "Don't think in ways that would offend God. Don't do things that will cause Him to punish you. Never offend Him, or a zap of lightning will certainly shoot from the sky and send you straight to hell." I shuddered at all the threats of damnation in the Bible. But were they just manufactured to scare us to death? What better way to stop people from thinking things through!

"That's how it works, Karen," he said gently. "They make you afraid to question. If you don't look too hard, they can keep the power."

"Daniel," I cried, "this is nothing more than a giant dysfunctional family . . . everyone is so scared of a father who has rage attacks that nobody dares to question him. Everyone loses their freedom to be themselves because they're terrified about what Dad might do!"

"It's an interesting comparison," he replied wryly. "Look at your New Testament. The early writers who were there with Jesus, and actually for many years after he left his body, tried to record the truth. People hurt them, even killed them sometimes. Then Jesus' words were changed all around so a few people could have all the power. It's really not hard to see how mixed up it is if you're not afraid to look."

"It isn't?" I was afraid of what he might say next. He was already bordering on saying the Bible was simply not true.

"Well, just look at what an awful story it is!" he said, as though it should be perfectly obvious. "Why would a God of love send his own son to suffer and to die in order to save the people from his own anger? Why wouldn't he just simply love and help them? Can you really accept the idea that God loves the son and loves the people so much that he kills one so he won't kill them all?" Daniel looked exasperated as he waited for my answer.

I had never thought about it like that! He was right; how could that story be true? And what about suffering? How could an almighty, loving God let little children die from horrible diseases? Why did floods and fires destroy life? The term "Act of God" had always puzzled me. I couldn't put it together with the words of disaster survivors: "Everyone around us was killed, but God saved our family. Our prayers were answered." What did that mean? God created the disaster in the first place and then allowed some people to perish while others were spared. What kind of a God was that? If a person acted that way, we'd lock him up as a psychopath!

I was struggling to find some answer to my dilemma. "Some people believe God does all these things as a test of our love . . . you know, like Job."

"Karen, how could a God of love send terrible pain to see if you will still love Him? The only thing that's created is fear, the opposite of love. You have lived for so long with the idea that if you displease God, He will send violent punishment. But your keepers continue to tell you this has to do with love! You can see how much confusion there is."

My mind had caught on a particular point. "Wait a minute; you said something really interesting. Daniel, isn't the opposite of love, hate?"

"No, Karen, it's fear, building up walls of density. That is what keeps you separated and alone. Did you know that the word 'sin' means to be apart from God, or to miss the mark? It has nothing to do with satisfying rules. Why would a loving God care about whether you follow a rule or not? Doesn't it seem awfully petty?"

My limbs felt numb, the beginning sign of shock, and I mutely nodded my head. "See, what has been distorted into rules that have to be followed in order to avoid the wrath of a terrible God was only meant to help people see how they could set down density. It's your free will to set it down, through one kind of action, or pick it up through another. The punishment comes out of the kind of reality that you make when you create more density, not out of the judgment of a god."

I thought about what I told clients who kept making the same mistakes over and over. They often felt they were somehow mentally or morally defective after the fourth marriage or the tenth lost job. I would remind them that results come from the actions they take. Therefore, if they didn't like the results they were getting in their lives, they needed to change the actions that were creating those results.

It had never occurred to me to look at the Bible, or other spiritual teachings, as sets of directions for creating reality. I always thought it was just "The Truth," and it was I who was always falling short. I certainly didn't consider these words as directions for living, for building communities and nations. But that's what they were. Daniel was saying our directions were all mixed up. Even if we followed them exactly, they flat out couldn't work!

"What about Satan?" I offered weakly, knowing I was about to see the last of my common belief system fall apart.

"More mixed-up teaching, I'm afraid," he said, confirming my suspicion. "Satan has come into reality because humans have created him. But he's just constructed out of density, the density inside people."

"So it's not Satan who's got us, but density? Density is created by us and we use it to create Satan. If we get rid of the density, there he goes. Off into oblivion!" This was a big relief. That had always been the threat. If I didn't follow God's rules, Satan was out there ready to get me. But Daniel was saying we had created our God out of our own energy! Once we got Him started, He took on a life of his own. All over the world, people had done the same thing, creating different gods out of different misunderstandings. Now those gods were out there influencing our lives, creating fear and controlling us. And through our fear and ignorance, we provided the energy to sustain them!

Now all the teachings were confused beyond recognition. It wasn't laziness about spiritual obedience that had the world in this mess, but reliance on scrambled messages. We had been doing the best we could with faulty information. No wonder so many people just gave up. People were leaving churches in droves. They were depressed, alienated, lost.

And nobody knew why! Not even the spiritual experts. They didn't understand any better than the rest of us. They inherited the same confusion and made institutions out of their misunderstanding. They kept these Earth gods going, worrying about ways to please them, looking up into the heavens for answers. Mankind had derailed along the way and needed to get back on track fast. Our adherence to a bunch of garbled messages had led to destruction. Earth's people were violent, diseased, hungry, and demoralized.

"Daniel, this is a tragedy, an awful series of catastrophic mistakes!" I held the sides of my head, trying to contain the truth quickly expanding past the confines of my skull.

He nodded his agreement.

A phrase from my Sunday school days went through my mind: "By its fruits you shall know it . . ." All the mixed-up teachings had produced was anguish, fear, and violence. Western civilization had been built on the Bible. Other cultures were following equally confused documents with tragic results. Tears rolled down my face as the enormity of our mistakes swept over me like a big unexpected wave.

The child looked at me, sorrow filling his eyes. "While people are busy falling to their knees and calling to their gods, they forget about the work they have to do. I'm so afraid if you don't begin to make choices to get rid of the density, your Earth will die."

❧ THIRTEEN ❧

The scent of flowers whispered across my face, and I found myself standing back in the field. The child who always seemed to be ahead of me was walking away. Scrambling after him, I called out, "The Earth may die? Daniel, isn't that a little strong? I mean, I know we aren't taking care of our resources very well and that pollution is pretty bad, but . . . die?"

I considered myself an environmentalist. I realized that Earth had finite resources and we'd better start taking good care of them. I lived in Idaho, after all. I had been witness to a terrible decline in the salmon population. People didn't seem to understand that we have to be careful about how we use the Earth so that the beauty could be enjoyed by everyone forever . . . but die? That sounded suspiciously like something a radical would say. We were entitled to use the resources of the Earth . . . that's what they were there for.

Daniel stopped and turned to me. "Yes, Karen. Die. See, with all of the increases in density, the Earth just can't support you. She was perfectly capable of taking care of you if you continued to set it down . . . but all these increases . . . it's not her fault, you know."

"Her . . . you mean Mother Nature . . . Mother Earth?"

"No, her . . . her, you know, Gaia," he said as if I should know. "When she came from heaven and built a body to support all of you, she had no idea you were going to make the choices you made. It's really not fair, you know. I'm not sure she ever would have volunteered for this if she had . . ."

I remember the exact moment when I lost my mind. Somehow, it just fell apart like the roses in my garden. Once they were dry, the slightest touch would send the petals to the ground. I could see Daniel's mouth moving. I could hear sounds, but they no longer made sense until he started calling my name.

"Karen . . . Karen . . ." His little face looked concerned. "I'm sorry. I went too fast. They warned me about that. Don't tell her too much. Human beings can't take it. They want to know, but they can't take it. It's like . . . well, we have an ocean to give you, but you only have a glass to receive it. Are you okay?"

My legs made an independent decision to let me fall to the ground. We were on a little slope. The air was warm and perfectly clear, and the birds rhapsodized in the tall trees. I allowed myself to sink into the soft grass, and looked over at the little boy with amazement. His forehead was furrowed, eyes intent.

"Are you okay?" he repeated. I did not know how to answer him. What did "okay" mean anymore?

I felt somehow innocent, stripped of the beliefs that normally bound my being. I was no longer interested in being courageous, intellectual, or even particularly grown-up. "Such as a little child shall enter the kingdom of heaven . . ." The words rang in my head, and they made sense to me for the first time.

"Daniel . . ." I whispered. "Can we just stay here for a little while? I mean, could we not blip off to somewhere else for a few minutes?"

"Sure!" he said enthusiastically. And then he vanished.

Too tired to be alarmed, I was grateful he had left me on firm ground this time. I stretched out and felt the fragrant earth send comforting arms up to meet me. I let go, just let go . . . for once in my life, I just let it all go.

I heard a voice off to my right somewhere. Drifting comfortably, I chose not to open my eyes. She seemed quite content to talk without my attention. Vaguely, I wondered if Daniel was coming back as I let myself float up and down on the current of her words . . .

"You see, Karen, you were all lost long ago and Gaia came to help you. Earth is not a solid lump of rock, but a living being with a body designed to nourish and sustain you. Just as you have a physical body inhabited by a spiritual being, so does Earth. Just look . . ."

I was having the most wondrous dream. A luminescent woman stood in front of me. Although she was very beautiful, it was her song that compelled me. A beautiful humming sound came from her and went through my skin, traveled through all of my organs, and landed softly in my heart. It seemed to explode in a thousand voices of love. I cried for the beauty of it. She reached out and I went toward her, knowing she had a gift for me. She opened her hands and there it was: Earth. So blue, so impossibly exquisite, it turned slowly. I could see particles of light flowing freely within this sphere; beautiful, sparkling light, unencumbered, increasing as I watched.

"Come home, Karen . . . please, come home . . ." she sang softly to me as I basked in her love.

"Going back to rejoin all the other beings is your right. There is a place where you belong, and where, in your absence, others grieve. Each of you has a place, a seat, if you will, that shall remain empty until you arrive. And each of you is waited for with all the love of the whole. And each of you is called . . . and sung to . . . and held . . . and sheltered . . . and wished for with the heart of the whole. There is no being among you who is disposable, no being who can truly be lost and not missed, for without you we are not whole. Do not think 'I do not matter,' for you matter as much as the totality of all itself."

I was awakened by my own sobs. Rolling over onto the warm earth, I let myself continue to cry. From deep inside, I knew I had not experienced a dream, but the truth. And in that moment, I cried for us all. My belly heaving against Gaia's body, I gave my tears to her, not knowing what else I could do.

﴾ FOURTEEN ﴿

"Time to get up! Come on . . . you get to be the one . . . you get to see . . . and I get to come, too!" I heard the voice calling to me from far away. He sounded so excited. How could anyone be so happy at this point?

"Daniel?" My eyelids felt permanently stuck together, and my mind judged that as a good state of affairs. I was afraid to open them, not sure I could take any more. Cracking one eye, I found his small face inches from mine.

"Hi," he said simply.

I quickly pushed myself back and sat up. "Why do you do these things?"

It was a rhetorical question. By now, I knew why he did these things; he liked to shock me, keep me off guard. It was as simple as that. But I needed some time to sort things out. When he took my hand as if to pull me to my feet I cried, "Stop! Just wait a minute!" My head hurt—tremendous pounding straight through my scalp. "Let me ask some questions . . . there's just been too much for me to take in."

He grinned back at me. "It's not so hard to understand. It's just like I said; everybody on Earth gets here, and then they forget and it takes them forever to remember. In the meantime, the Earth can't take it any more and . . ."

"Wait. Just wait a second. Let me just stop and think." I shook my head slightly to one side, as though the motion might settle my brain cells in a more comfortable position. "Daniel . . . the Earth . . . Gaia. It's—she's alive? Was that real? What I saw—was that real?"

He looked over at me, and his smile of affirmation was like the sun coming up. "Daniel, who are you anyway?"

"That's not important at all!" he said, laughing. "The real question is, who are you?"

I decided to be concise about what I had gathered thus far. "Well, from what I can figure out, I'm a human being who is terribly confused about herself, the world, and the nature of reality, just like the rest of the people on Earth."

"That's good!"

"Confusion is good?" Another of my common-sense rules was out the window.

"It is a good start," he said with his usual maddening good humor. "Confusion is the first sign of letting go of what you always thought was absolute truth."

It's also the first sign of mental illness, Alzheimer's, and a lot of other terrible things, I thought. My head was still pounding.

"Would you like me to fix your headache?" Daniel asked brightly.

"That'd be great," I said, pushing against my temples in vain. "But I don't suppose you have any aspirin; I can't concentrate with this pain."

He placed his small hands on my head and whispered, "Just let me be with you. Let me come in."

He was so gentle, I closed my eyes and momentarily forgot to hold on to my fear. Why not let down my defenses with him? My world had already come unglued. What more could he do to me?

"That's it. Just let go." I relaxed into my heart and knew I was safe. Instantly, my headache went away.

My eyes flew open. "How did you do that?"

He shrugged and replied, "Just helped you again with your density. You were just scared about all the stuff you've been learning, and you fell right back in the mud."

"And that gave me a headache?" I asked, surprised that density had anything to do with physical pain.

He said, matter-of-factly, "Any time you get sick it's because of density, you know. Your energy gets divided, like I was telling you before. When that happens, parts of your body start to suffocate. Just like when air gets cut off and you can't breathe. When parts of your body are cut off from energy, they start to hurt and sometimes they even start to die off."

What he said made sense to me, but I knew our medical system had no idea about density. Reading my mind, Daniel responded, "Your doctors are great at following what happens to people's bodies while they suffocate from density. But they don't know a thing about how a body can get better when a person decides to free it from all that thickness, and doctors often don't have any idea why something they give to a sick person works. They are surprised when the person gets better. It's a good thing they don't want anybody to know that they don't know what happened. If the doctor acted surprised, the person could get sick all over again, because he falls back into density . . . the kind of density that has to do with fear and doubt."

"Are you saying people cure themselves?" I asked, half hoping it was true. After all, if density could make us sick, then knowing about it could make us well again.

"Well, lots of people get better even if the doctor just gives them sugar pills. Just shows how people heal themselves when they get their energy flowing, get past their fear, and believe they will get better. I think that's really important, don't you?"

I had never thought about it like that. Why did we so easily dismiss apparent healing of the physical body in response to an inert substance as merely the placebo effect? After all, the person did get well somehow. And what exactly did spontaneous remission mean? Daniel was saying that people healed themselves when they believed they were going to get better. It had to do with density and energy flow.

What had happened seemed so simple. My pain was totally gone. "Daniel . . . my head really does feel completely better. Tell me some more about how energy and healing go together."

"Okay," he said, and then fumbled for a good way to explain it. "Well, let's see . . . it's like this . . . no, that's not a good example . . . well . . . let's see, no . . . oh, just look!"

ꙮ FIFTEEN ꙮ

My eyes had involuntarily closed. The words "just look" had come to mean something radical was about to occur. In this moment, I was sure I wasn't up to dealing with whatever it was.

The little boy's voice sounded suspiciously cheerful, "Karen . . . Karen . . . come on . . . open your eyes! You can do it. I want you to see!"

It was dark here. Completely black. "Daniel . . ." My voice was shaking, I was deeply afraid that he might not be by my side. "Daniel . . . are you there?"

"Of course I'm here. Where else would I be?" His tone implied that he had remained unfailingly by my side.

"Where are we?" I asked quietly, barely willing to turn my head.

"It's really something, don't you think?" Daniel's merry voice seemed incongruous with the setting. This place seemed terribly serious. I had never been especially afraid of the dark, but this was so completely silent and black, so devoid of anything.

I looked up in time to see a bright light coming straight at us. "Look out!" I cried, ducking as a sphere about the size of a basketball flew past at rapid speed.

"Pretty wonderful, don't you think?" Daniel said enthusiastically.

"How can you say that?" I was carefully surveying the horizon for another dangerous . . . another dangerous . . . what the hell was that?

"Here comes another one," Daniel said quietly. "Isn't it beautiful?"

Terrified, I looked out across the darkness and saw nothing. "I don't see anything, Dan—" I fell to my knees as the ball of light came toward me faster than anything I had ever seen.

Panic set in. "Daniel . . . please help me. Where are we? I want out of here." Hysteria was unbecoming, but impossible to avoid. "Get me out of this place!"

He sounded very disappointed, "But I want you to see . . . you said you wanted to understand about healing."

"Healing?" I choked the word out through clenched teeth. "Healing? Are you out of your mind?" I was glad I had remained on my knees as another spinning ball zoomed into view and headed right for us.

"Well, how are you going to know how to feel better if you don't understand this place? Just watch." He spoke calmly as the unidentified flying object went over our heads.

I didn't want to watch anything anymore at any time, ever again. Nonetheless, I knew my best chance to get out of this godforsaken place was to follow his instructions.

I could hear my breath coming and going like that of a wild animal caught in a cage. "Okay, okay, I can't see anything. What do you want me to watch?"

"Watch the sphere," he said quietly. My heart lurched as another bright light appeared out of nowhere. "Don't panic this time. Just concentrate for a minute." The ball headed for us at supersonic speed.

"Concentrate? Concentrate on what?" I cried as I threw myself down.

"Well, concentrate on what you want it to do, of course."

"I want it to stop!" I screamed.

"Just concentrate, Karen," he repeated. "Tell it to stop."

"Stop! Stop! Stop!" I yelled, bringing every particle of strength I had into the command. The ball of light stopped.

"That's good!" Daniel said like a father whose second-grader had finally managed to hit the baseball.

Suspended in the darkness, the sphere turned slowly. It seemed to be waiting for further instructions.

"Well, what do you want it to do now?" Daniel asked brightly.

"I want it to go away," I said with a mixture of fatigue and desperation.

"So tell it to go away."

"Go away," I said with little enthusiasm. Nothing happened. I looked over at Daniel with renewed fear. "What do I do now? It didn't work."

"Well, how can you expect anything to happen if you don't apply any feeling to what you say?"

"What's feeling have to do with it?" I asked, watching the globe with the kind of wariness prompted by seeing a bee making its way across the windshield of my car in heavy traffic.

He heaved a sigh. "How is he supposed to know what to pay attention to if you don't care about it?"

"He? He? The ball is a he?" My voice sounded like a rusty door hinge.

Daniel's laughter filled the silence, "Of course the ball isn't a he . . . I was talking about the guy who runs this place!"

⋐ SIXTEEN ⋑

At last report, my mind had fallen apart like the spent petals of a rose; now those petals spiraled chaotically as if down a street in a swift wind.

"Runs this place . . . ?" I was dumbfounded by the sight of a man appearing out of the darkness. Enormous, he held the still-spinning ball of light in his hands. His azure eyes were luminous and calm, and he looked at me as if waiting for something.

"Well, tell him what to do!" Daniel's voice seemed far away. This man was beautiful in his simplicity. Clear light seemed to shine from his face. His eyes were filled with devotion.

"I don't know what you mean," I whispered.

"That's what he's waiting for . . . you know, for you to tell him what to do with the energy."

"You mean the ball . . . that's energy?" I said lamely.

"Well, of course!" As an afterthought, he added, "What did you think it was?"

I felt apologetic about my ignorance. "Daniel . . . please try to remember, I don't know anything. Who is this person?"

I looked at his gentle face. It seemed he would do anything I asked.

"I'm sorry," he said, bailing me out of my embarrassment. "I keep forgetting that you've forgotten everything. That's so weird how it works . . . why you forget and everything . . . personally, I think things would go a lot better if you remembered in the first place. Do you have any idea how much time gets wasted in this forgetting thing? I mean . . . "

"Daniel, please!" The giant man in front of me had reached out his hand and caught another globe of light. His eyes held renewed expectation. "Who is this man? Where are we? Why is he waiting for me to tell him what to do with the energy?"

"Well, who else would tell him?" Daniel sounded genuinely confused.

"Why me? I don't know him, or anything about this place." I was a little annoyed. The man was beginning to remind me of a Labrador retriever I had when I was about fifteen. The dog would sit at my feet and look up at me with absolute dedication and love. He would wait forever for one word, one pat on the head from me. That was a special kind of love.

The little boy threw out his arms and dropped his next bomb. "Karen . . . for heaven's sake . . . of course you have to tell him what to do. He belongs to you, and so does that energy! How else could your body run?"

"Body? Did you say body?" I felt dizzy; what did this being have to do with my body?

"Where do you think we are?" He looked at me innocently. "We're inside your body! And that's your nature spirit. All human beings have one. When your body first starts up, you know, when you come to Earth, you have to have a body to use while you're here. Anyway, it's his job to construct the body and to keep it all running. He does that with energy . . . a special kind of energy that only a nature spirit has!"

I was stunned. He continued, "Isn't it good that you don't have to worry about your heart beating and your food getting digested and all that stuff? That would really be a pain if you had to say, 'beat' for all one hundred thousand times your heart beats every twenty-four hours. What if you had to tell yourself all the time to stay at ninety-eight-point-six degrees? That would keep you up all night! And what if you had to worry about remembering to create all seven million new red blood cells that appear every second? A person should be really grateful to their nature spirit. What would you do without him?"

"I don't know what to tell him to do with that energy." I said weakly.

"Well, why don't you tell him to send it through your system freely and smoothly? Then you won't be so tired! Of course, he's going to have to fight through the clutter of the density you've got going to do that, but ask anyway."

As if by thought transference, as soon as I agreed to do as Daniel suggested, the man threw the spheres forward, and spiraling beautifully, they disappeared from sight. I felt a wave of energy sweep through me. Suddenly, I was invigorated and ready to understand more.

"All this time, I've had a nature spirit just waiting for me to tell him what to do with the energy?" My heart was pounding with excitement. "Where does the energy come from?"

"It depends a lot on what you eat, the air you take in, the water you drink. When you eat animals, instead of giving you energy, your nature spirit has to defend against the fear and anguish that comes in. Did you know that? The way animals die so that people can eat them makes them terribly afraid. That energy is what you take in when you eat meat. And water, by the time you drink it, is full of chemicals. And air. Besides all the pollution, most people don't seem to really breathe. They take air in little short gasps, way up high in their chest. Watch sometimes. See how many take a full breath, all the way down into their bellies."

Watching the beautiful man in front of me, I asked, "Does he listen all the time . . . I mean, about what we want him to do with the energy?"

"Of course he does!" Daniel answered. "He can't choose by himself. He loves you so much, he just waits for you to tell him. It's just, well, he's kind of simple. He gets confused a lot. If you keep repeating something, even if you don't really mean it, even if it hurts you in the end, he will do it because you told him to do it. So you have to be careful about what you say."

I thought for a moment. "How can we be careful if we don't even know he's there? Do you mean he listens to everything . . . all the time?"

"Yep," he nodded. "That's his job—to run your body just the way you tell him. So watch out when you keep saying your job is a pain in the neck, or your back is breaking. He even listens to people saying over and over that they aren't good enough, or big enough, to do things. Sometimes he just starts making more cells so they'll be enough . . . people end up with what you call cancer. He doesn't mean to hurt you. It's just, like I said, he's kind of simple."

I continued to gaze at the man in front of me. He had captured another two spheres and seemed again to be waiting for me to tell him what to do. "Daniel, how does he know about making my heart beat without my telling him? I don't think I've ever even thought about it particularly, let alone asked for it to go ahead and beat."

"He knows that from the basic pattern he got in the first place. The one that was given to him when you came here. I'd tell him to send some of that energy he's holding through you. You still look a little tired."

"How in the world would you expect me to feel after all of this? Of course I'm tired!"

He met my frustration with some of his own. "That's what I've been trying to tell you. People keep thinking they feel sick or tired because of stuff going on outside themselves. But it's not about that at all. It's what you tell him to do with the energy and how much energy you give him to use and, of course, how much density you've got blocking your energy pathways. You can change it because you created it in the first place!"

"I did?"

"Well, sure!" he answered. "Give your nature spirit a name, talk to him directly. Give him what he needs to do what you ask. It's all yours for the asking!"

The man was so beautiful, incandescent, his eyes filled with love, as he continued to wait for me. "Okay, let's see, what's a fitting name? Adam . . . I'll call him Adam. Adam, please send the energy you are holding through my system." Instantly, the spheres zoomed past me and I felt wonderful.

"That's so cool!" I found myself exclaiming. "You mean all this time, every time I've battled fatigue, all I needed to do was ask?"

"Yep," he said with a nod. "Well, ask and supply him with the materials he needs to make beautiful energy and clear out the density. That'll do it for you. The pattern you were given in the first place wasn't for a body that was supposed to be tired or sick. The purpose of this lifetime required a strong body pattern. Sometimes, it's better for your work on Earth to use some other kind of pattern, even a pattern that will make for a short lifetime, or . . ."

As he rambled on, my mind caught on a piece of information like a jacket sleeve snared on a branch in the woods. "Daniel, you keep using the word 'pattern' . . . something I was given to use when I came here. Came from where? What are you talking about?"

꧁ SEVENTEEN ꧂

"I hate my body. Why can't I do something about my weight?
God, I'm so fat . . . there's Judy, she looks great, why can't I get
it together? What should I do about the house payment? If I
send it now, it will get there early and I could get the interest
in the account for a few more . . . Boy, I wish I were already
home . . . I hate my body, I wish I were a little taller. That guy
sure looks good . . . God, I don't like the way my business is
going, I wonder if some more advertising would be useful . . .
Did I close the garage door before I left? I'm so hungry. Can't
I ever just do without food for a little while? No wonder I look
like this. A sandwich sounds good, and a donut . . . Why are
you like this? Look at that guy, he must eat the right things all
the time . . . If I could just get it together . . . I wonder if the car
needs to be serviced, have to remember to check when I get
home . . . Maybe next year I can buy that house I saw the other
day . . . Boy, I don't like Linda. She's so petty, so cheap. I don't
even like the way she looks . . . What if we don't have enough
money? What am I going to do . . . I don't like Kelly either . . .
She really bugs me . . . the way she criticizes everybody . . . God,
I'm so fat, my pants are too tight . . . A chicken salad sandwich
sounds good . . . Did I set the sprinkler system?"

To my amazement, another figure had appeared out of the
darkness. A small woman, she seemed powered by nervous en-

ergy. Moving in circles, she talked rapidly, seemingly unaware of our presence.

Adam seemed deeply affected by this stranger as she continued with sentences which did not seem to connect with one another. "What if I can't pay my bills? If everyone would just do it the way I tell them to, we wouldn't be in this mess . . . I need to go past the dry cleaner and pick up my . . . won't fit . . . I hate this body . . . Maybe an oak tree would grow in that area next to . . . I wonder if they can get the spots out of the upholstery . . . Business, what can I do to bring in some more business? . . ."

"Daniel," I whispered, "who is that? Adam seems upset." "Upset" was not the right word. Adam was cringing as the stranger circled around him. The light that had infused him was dimming. He seemed smaller somehow. Several spheres of energy were in his hands, but he seemed confused about what to do. As Adam began to cry, his body bent over and the spheres fell to his feet unnoticed.

The woman quickly grabbed a few of the balls and rasped, "Give me those!" Adam's sorrow seemed as deep as the ocean. He began to sway, and I was afraid he was going to crumple to the ground.

"We've got to do something!" I said urgently. "That woman's destroying Adam!"

"She's a really unfortunate creation, don't you think?" Daniel said sadly. "There's really no purpose to her at all. She's just another product of the awful misunderstandings you all have. I'll try to help, but watch what happens." With that, he approached the frenetic woman.

"You know, everything is perfectly all right," he said very quietly. The woman did not acknowledge his existence, but continued to ramble. Daniel persisted in trying to gain the woman's attention, now moving with her as she ran in circles. "It's all right to calm down."

"I wish someone else would take some responsibility around here . . . I guess I should get the dogs' teeth cleaned. They say it adds years to their lives. I should get my own teeth cleaned . . . It's hard to read the numbers on our house, I'll have to fix that . . . The gutters . . . if I don't get them cleaned out, water isn't going to drain where it's supposed to and we could have real problems . . . I hate my body, I wonder how much Glen makes . . . I'm hungry. Some chips would taste good."

I looked at the scene in front of me. The giant nature spirit had become a tragic figure, sobbing and frightened, unable to cope with the spheres of light. The insane stranger seemed to gain more energy as she talked, moving faster and faster. The little boy was caught up in trying to get her attention, so far without any success.

I jumped back involuntarily when Daniel suddenly shouted, "Stop! Just stop for a second!"

The woman came to an abrupt halt, astonishment widening her eyes and stopping her speech. She took a deep breath and started moving again. "I can't stop. What would happen? Who would take responsibility? Everyone else can stop, but I have so much to do. When I get everything all done, perhaps I will stop. But there's too much to do! If Brad would just do what he says he will do, I could stop. But I hate my body . . . I wonder if the driveway needs to be resurfaced . . . Maybe a cold beer . . . No, that's too many calories . . . I should get those Shakespeare tickets before they sell out . . . What can I do to get some additional money coming in? . . . I should have taken time to run today . . ."

"Daniel, do something!" I was desperate to help Adam. This stranger was repulsive, oblivious to the pain she was causing.

"Stop! Stop!" I found myself crying out. "Please, stop! Can't you see what you're doing to Adam?"

I ran in front of the woman, who stopped speaking for a moment and then began again. "I have work to do, lots of work to do. I'm responsible for so much. There should be more time in the day. Got to keep moving." She could barely breathe as the random words continued to flow. Trying to get around me, she seemed desperate to keep walking. I insisted on blocking her way and she looked at me with fear, like an animal trapped in someone's headlights. Suddenly, she changed. "You should feel sorry for me. After all, I have to do everything. Without my work, what would happen around here?"

"Things would go a lot better!" I blurted, feeling completely justified in my attack.

"Good! Oh, Karen, that's so good!" I was surprised by Daniel's enthusiasm. After all, I hadn't done anything anyone else wouldn't have done. This woman was out of control. She had to be stopped before she destroyed poor Adam.

"Better . . . better, you say? Things would go out of control . . . I'm in charge of everything. Without me, there would be a horrible mess. People would find out about how much we don't know. People would discover our secrets . . . you know, all the things we don't know how to do. It's my job to make sure nobody finds out who I really am. They wouldn't like me, you know . . . I wonder how many calories are in one chocolate chip cookie? Do you think there are more in frozen yogurt? I really do need to get back to work. I hate my body." Off she went again, this time running in a figure-eight pattern.

"Stop her, Daniel!" I didn't know what to do next. I had given it my best shot.

"You stop her, Karen!" the little boy shouted. "Come on, you can do it!"

I looked over at Daniel and cried, "I don't know how! What can I do? She's so determined!"

I was tremendously frustrated as I saw the woman steal another sphere from Adam. This was an awful experience. I didn't want to be one of those people who watches someone being mugged on the street and does nothing. Adam didn't seem able to protect himself at all.

I felt a familiar surge of adrenaline. "All right! That's enough!" My voice surprised me. Sounding like General MacArthur, my tone conveyed the unequivocal message that what I said was going to happen, period, end of discussion. Moses probably sounded like that, I thought as the woman stopped, looking completely confused.

"That's good!" Daniel cried out. "Karen, that's so good!" Why was this little boy always so pleased with things that were out of character for me? Every time I behaved in a way that was completely unusual for me, he was overjoyed. I'll have to ask him about that, I thought as I continued with my MacArthur impression, "Stop hurting Adam! Knock it off and get the hell out of here!"

To my horror, the woman sat down and started to cry. "Damn!" I muttered. "I didn't expect her to do that. What should I do now?"

Daniel whispered his reply. "Karen, don't let her get away with that. If you let her, she'll just do the same thing in a different way. Tell her you know what she's up to!"

"But I don't!" Now I was confused. "I don't even know who she is, let alone what she's up to."

The woman began another soliloquy, "Nobody understands how hard it is, I'm responsible for everything . . . I don't like how I'm treated. After all, what would happen without me . . . I keep all the secrets . . . I get everything done and I work very,

very hard . . . I deserve better than this . . . If they would just look at it my way, then . . ."

To my astonishment, she suddenly jumped up and snatched another sphere from Adam. "That's mine!" she snarled.

"I said stop!" The words came from deep inside me, powered by an intensity I had seldom known. The woman promptly sat down and looked balefully in my direction. "That's incredible," I muttered to Daniel. "Give her any room at all and she takes off!"

"Yep." The little boy gazed at the woman, who now looked like her plug had been pulled. "Look at Adam," he said softly.

Light began to course through Adam's body. Soon he was filled with the power of a river approaching the sea. Rods of gorgeous, iridescent light shot out from his hands, and a magnificent smile further illuminated his face.

"Thank God we got that horrible person under control! How can we make sure she doesn't start up again? Who is she, anyway?"

Daniel began to giggle. "Who do you think she is, Karen?" His eyes danced as he waited for my answer.

"I don't know! How would I know? Why do you insist on expecting me to automatically understand things I have no experience with?" He could be absolutely maddening, I thought as he continued to laugh. "Come on, Daniel. Just tell me who she is."

Up went the little arms in a familiar exuberant gesture. "She's you, of course! Who else could she be?" And he disappeared again.

ᥬ EIGHTEEN ᥫ

"Me!" I was astounded by Daniel's answer. And more importantly, my feelings were hurt. I wasn't like that woman at all. I would never behave that way. She was so out of control. Caught up in my reaction to the little boy's unexpected insult, I did not notice my surroundings.

"Well, not really you, just what you think is you," the familiar voice said.

I looked up, expecting to see Daniel. I was standing on a magnificent black beach. Black sand, this must be Hawaii, I thought. Good. I can cope with that. I'll worry about how I got here later. "Where are you, Daniel?" I called out.

"Right here," he replied, but I could see nothing but empty beach.

I loved Hawaii. Once you moved away from Waikiki, there was something so magical about the islands. For a moment, I peacefully watched the aquamarine waves greet the beach. The air here was so pure, flowers and salt water blending together in an ancient perfume. I took a deep breath and sank my feet into the warm sand. "Okay, Daniel. Come out, wherever you are."

"I'm right here. Just like I said." Out of the corner of my eye, I saw him approaching. Wearing nothing but bright red swimming trunks, he looked like any other little kid ready for a day at the beach.

He'd better put on some sunscreen, I thought before I realized it was a ridiculous concept. This child could disappear at will. Somehow, his white skin would survive the tropical sun without the assistance of modern chemistry. "I don't think it was very nice to say that awful woman was me. I'm not anything like that!" I said, my hurt feelings coming back. "Why did you say that? Who was she, really?"

"Like I said, she's you . . . or at least she's what you think of as you."

"Okay" I said wearily. "Do we have to play another game? Why are you telling me she's me when clearly she's not?"

He looked at me very seriously, sunshine bouncing off his blond hair. "Think about it, Karen. Isn't that what you think you are? Day to day, isn't that what goes on in your mind?"

I thought for a moment as I watched the waves. "Well, there are some similarities. I do think about my responsibilities . . . I do have a business to run and a lot of things to take care of . . . and, I do wish I were a little thinner. But I'm not like that woman."

"Yep, you are . . . that's you!" Daniel ran across the sand toward the water, his little legs pumping hard. He reached the water and began to play, splashing happily, oblivious to my discomfort. "Come on, Karen. Let's play!"

"We don't have time to play," I called out irritably. "We have to get back. I have too much to do. Maybe someday, when everything's under control at work and at home . . . there are too many things to be concerned about to just waste time playing . . ."

"See!" He looked at me intently, a piece of seaweed draped over one ear. "That's what you think of as you. That stuff goes on all the time in your mind . . . what you have to do, what you're responsible for, what other people think of you."

"But . . ."

"And you shouldn't keep saying you hate your body. That really makes Adam upset!"

"Adam? I'm the one who saved Adam! I wouldn't do anything to upset him," I protested.

"You're right, Karen. He doesn't deserve that. You did save him. That was really good. But you also abuse him. And that's not good at all. Keep doing that, and he can't give you what you need. Pretty soon, you get sick and worn down and then . . . well, you know what happens then."

"No, what happens then?" How was I supposed to know?

"You die, of course . . ." He ran off down the beach while I battled my anxiety. I decided to sit down for a while. If it was true that Adam was in charge of my body, it made sense that the crazy woman belonged to me as well. And I could see what kind of an impact that woman had on Adam. I remembered how he had let several spheres fall to the ground. If that happened often enough, I supposed I would run out of energy. Besides, if Adam was in charge of all my body systems, he'd better not be distracted like that.

"See, Karen . . ." I jumped as Daniel came up behind me. How did he do that? Just a moment ago, he was several hundred yards down the beach.

"See, that woman is what you end up with when something really wonderful gets all messed up!"

"Okay, I give up. What do you mean?" At least we weren't someplace weird. I consoled myself with that thought. Hawaii was perfectly normal. We weren't standing in midair, we weren't inside my body, we hadn't traveled down into a plant. This was good. Hawaii. I liked Hawaii.

"Well, as I was saying before, when you decide to come here, you send your nature spirit out to start constructing a body for you. You also send out another spirit. Its job is to help you find the information that your soul sent you to the Earth to gather up. It's really cool, it just looks out peacefully and collects what you need. It gets along really well with Adam, which is good because you can see he's really sensitive . . . so, if you can just let it do what it's . . ."

Daniel had plopped down beside me and kept talking. Unfortunately, my mind had made a decision to stop like an unwilling horse does in the hands of an inept rider. "Wait! Hold it! Came from where? Another spirit? How many of these spirits do I have!" I shook my head, hoping the movement would somehow arrange these pieces of information in an acceptable form.

"Three," he said simply, and watched for my reaction.

"Three?" I whispered, knowing he was not going to retract his original statement. "Daniel, I was always taught we had one spirit."

Actually, that wasn't precisely true. I had heard from one source or another that there was no such thing as spirit at all—we were carbon-based units set to self destruct at 7.2 decades . . . I had never really believed that. But three spirits? What was he talking about?

"Yep," he said. "And they're all beautiful when they're left to be what they are. But people forget so fast, and then they get all confused and the next thing you know, you've got a sick Adam, a really mean woman, and the other one can't even find a way to talk to you anymore."

"The other one?" I quickly pleaded, "Please, please, please let's not go anywhere for a little while. Let's just stay here and take it nice and slow."

"Okay," he agreed, shrugging his small shoulders. "You know that mean woman doesn't really mean to be mean, if you know what I mean . . ."

I'm still in the hands of an incomprehensible person, I thought, panic beginning to rise. What's going to happen to me?

Just breathe, take in this lovely beach. Calm down. After all you've been through, it can't get much worse. Relax . . . breathe.

"That's good, Karen! Take in some air and tell Adam to just slow everything down for you."

"Daniel . . . am I going to be all right?" I needed to hear it, even if I didn't believe it.

"Oh, Karen, I sure hope so . . ." he answered, looking very worried.

"That's not very reassuring."

"Well, it's all up to you. You're the only one who can help yourself." He looked up at me with those beautiful eyes.

"But I didn't get myself into this situation," I said, continuing to protest. "I mean, I was riding along in an airplane and you showed up. Next thing I know, I've lost my mind!"

"But that's the problem, Karen, you haven't yet lost your mind. I wish you would. It wasn't supposed to be there in the first place!"

"Wait! What do you mean? I wasn't supposed to have a mind?" What could he mean? I had to have a mind; how else could I function, think, know anything? The thought of losing it was really scary. They'll find me mumbling on a street somewhere. I won't be able to work. I'll lose my house. I won't have any control over myself.

"See, that's exactly how she does it!" Daniel shouted from the water. "That's exactly how that mean woman convinces you to keep her around. But she messes everything up . . . just the opposite of what you think!"

I walked slowly toward the child. "But Daniel, how would I be without a mind? You know, 'I think, therefore I am.'" I stuck my toes in the water, convinced I was losing my mind,

"You'd use your other mind . . . the one that works," he replied matter-of-factly.

"My other mind?" Funny what becomes important when you're under severe stress. I suddenly became very concerned about what I was wearing. My outfit was not at all appropriate for the beach. I surveyed my long, corduroy pants and flannel shirt. I had been on my way to Seattle, looking perfectly normal. If anyone sees me out here, they're going to call the loony bin and demand an immediate pickup.

"See! She's at it again . . . worrying about what other people are going to think about you. That's how she talks you into letting her stay."

"So, you're telling me that the woman who was torturing Adam is my mind . . . some kind of mind that I wasn't supposed to have, and should get rid of, but I have another mind that works?" That sounded absolutely crazy. I was going to lose my license when I got back to Idaho. Crazy people are not allowed to be counselors . . . well, at least they shouldn't be allowed to be counselors. If I lost my ability to work, it would be a disaster. Somehow, I had to get things under control.

"There she goes again! You've got to stand up, Karen. Don't let her get away with that!"

"Daniel," I said wearily, "where did this mind come from?"

"Other people," he answered. "Right from the start, when you're in a little baby body, they start creating that mean woman. Actually, we can call her your social mind. Your social mind gets filled with judgments and opinions. They teach it to compare you to other people all the time. They tell it you don't know anything, you're just a weak nobody who can't do a thing for herself. They teach you your body is some kind of machine, instead of helping you to remember Adam. And they make you totally forget where you came from and who you really are."

"They? Who are they? Do you mean parents? Wait a minute! Lots of people have really wonderful parents. It can't be all their fault."

"Yes, many people have wonderful parents, Karen," he said gently. "But the thing is, those parents didn't remember either. Their parents provided them with a social mind, too. And then, their social mind teaches their children to have one. If you had children, you would have taught them to have one, too. Isn't that sad?"

"I guess I don't understand how it should have been." I was finished pretending I knew anything at all.

"Well," he continued, "if your parents had remembered, they could have helped you to not forget right from the start. They would have known that they helped to provide you with a body, but you were someone beyond that. They were just supposed to protect you while your body was little. You never belonged to them, and it was never their job to mold you, or train you, or do anything to you. They didn't mean to create a social mind, but they didn't know what else to do. They thought you were empty when you got here, but you were full! You were full right from the start!"

"Full?" What did that mean?

"Yep . . . full of intelligence, not the book kind, but the kind that runs the Universe." His voice grew tender. "And love—Karen, you were so filled with love."

"That's certainly different from the way most of us see babies. They look so helpless."

"Just because they can't control their new bodies very well for a while doesn't mean they're empty," Daniel said. "Anyway, their nature spirit gets a lot done in a short time. Nine months isn't much time to build all those cells and systems. By the time they get to a first birthday, they've learned a lot about how to move around!"

"Well, what do you think parents should be doing, Daniel?" This was so strange. I was playing in the water with this little boy, asking him how parents should behave. How should he know?

He looked at me and smiled. "Reminding you from the start who you really are. Telling you about Adam and your other two spirits, helping you remember where you came from and why . . . that kind of stuff." With that, he scooped water up in his hands and tossed it at me. Giggling, he looked so little, and yet he had already taught me so much. Maybe we had it all backward. Maybe the kids were supposed to teach the grown-ups.

Ignoring the showers of seawater sent my way, I asked, "So, you're saying this social mind is really like some kind of implant that comes from outside me?"

"Yep." He stopped to examine me.

"From other people's ideas about the world, it comes from other people's experiences and beliefs, not really mine?" I didn't like how this was beginning to sound.

"Well, some of the experiences are yours. But remember when I was talking about how you only see what you already know?"

"Well, yes."

"So all you do is collect experiences that agree with what other people have already given you. That's all you notice. Pretty soon, your social mind has all the power, and you don't even know it's there!"

"Why is it like that? Why does it behave that way?" Maybe this was really a part of me after all. I had a sinking feeling.

"It's scared, that's all," Daniel said sadly.

"Scared? Scared of what?"

"Getting ended."

It made no sense to me. "Getting ended?"

"Yep," he answered. "If you ever start to look at it carefully, you'll decide to stop giving it energy. If you do, it'll end. So it gets scared a lot. Unfortunately, there's not much reason for it to feel that way, 'cause you never look anyway."

I felt accused. "How could I look if I didn't even know it was there?"

"That's true," he said. "I keep forgetting you don't remember anything." He shook his head. "Wow, that's so weird how that works!"

"Daniel . . . how did this happen to us? How did we get so terribly mixed up?"

I thought about what he had said about comparisons. If I thought about it, my whole life was about comparisons. How did I look? How was I doing financially? Was my home nice enough? Did people like me? It was all about competition and posturing. In truth, when I felt really good it was usually because I had measured up to some standard. Did I really have an obnoxious, constantly judging mean-spirited part of me inside? You bet I did.

"It steals, too." Daniel interrupted my ruminations.

"Huh?"

"It steals every chance it gets," Daniel repeated.

"What do you mean?" Oh, God, it was worse than I thought. Was I stealing without knowing it?

"Everybody's social mind does the same thing," he continued. "See, it wants as much power as it can get. It robs Adam first. But after that, it robs anybody else it can."

"I don't understand."

His eyes were bright. "Karen, I bet you can think of times when you've been with someone and felt really drained afterward. Can you?"

"Sure, Daniel," I answered. "Some people are pretty challenging."

"You get so tired because their social mind gets in and takes energy away from Adam," he said.

I was shocked. "What?"

"Well," he said softly, "all the social minds are pretty much out of control. They do what they want. They even talk to each other. And then it gets really confusing for people."

"Talk to each other?"

"Yep. While you are talking to another person, your two social minds talk to each other. Sometimes what the social minds say doesn't agree with what you say out loud. Have you ever just not liked somebody, and not been able to figure out why?"

"Well, yes." I liked to think of myself as an accepting person, but there were lots of people I really didn't like without good reason.

He continued his instruction. "That's because the two social minds have said stuff to each other that's not nice at all. They might be attacking each other, trying to steal energy, while you're having a regular conversation."

I thought about those interactions that seemed to go wrong for no reason at all. Two nice people just at odds with each other. Sometimes not so subtle odds.

Daniel looked at me intently. "Yep, just two social minds struggling away, and you never know it!" Off he skipped down the beach.

"Wait, Daniel!" No wonder people have such a hard time getting along! We don't even know what we're saying to each other . . . doesn't that get people killed sometimes? I mean, if I'm asking for directions and insulting the person at the same time, things could get ugly fast. And wars; how can we get to world peace with these idiots talking away without our knowledge? "How do we stop the social minds?"

"By being like them." Daniel stopped and pointed up the beach. I had left my glasses on the airplane. What looked like two brown paper bags seemed to be approaching.

"Them? You mean there are people in Hawaii who don't have social minds?" I thought he had said all human beings were in the same mess. "How did they escape, Daniel?"

"They didn't," he said quietly. "They aren't here anymore."

"But I can see them now."

The two men had become more clear. Brown and muscular, they were headed straight toward us. They smiled, and there was something different about them. They seemed radiant. That's what living in paradise can do for you, I thought. They looked so healthy. Actually, they were quite beautiful.

"What do you mean, they aren't here anymore?"

"Well, they're here, but not there," Daniel said, grinning up at the new arrivals.

There was something odd about these two guys, but I couldn't put my finger on it. They seemed so full. They didn't seem to need anything at all. That was an interesting revelation. Most people need something from you. Most people had a social mind that needed energy. Everybody I talked to needed energy. But these two didn't.

What a different feeling it was to be near them. Somehow, they were giving to me. I could feel it. Their presence was making me feel better, stronger, more safe. As I looked at them, I was aware of something rising from my feet, through my legs, through my lower body, up into my chest. It was warm, nurturing, fulfilling, peaceful.

"God! How do you do that?" I whispered, feeling incomprehensibly grateful. It dawned on me that what I was feeling was a tangible form of love. They were offering love, and somehow I could feel its energy. This wasn't conceptual love. This was literally an offering of energy, freely given, mine to have.

"Thank you," I breathed, my eyes wide as my body continued to fill with the wonderful energy.

"That's what Jesus meant when he said to love each other,"

Daniel said brightly. "He meant give each other the energy of love, not just ideas about love. You just have to do what they're doing, and things could be a whole lot better!"

I was bursting with the delicious feeling. "Why did you say they weren't here? They certainly are!"

"Well, they're here, but not there." He didn't make any sense at all.

"Huh?"

"Well, just look!" There were those words again. But I was now eager to look. Whatever I had to see to explain the wonderful experience I had just had with these two strangers, I wanted to see. But nothing could have possibly prepared me for what happened next.

❧ NINETEEN ❧

The sky had gone softly gray, and the sea was dark as charcoal. I was calm inside, filled with the energies of love. The two mysterious men seemed long gone now as the warm wind brushed my face. The little child stood by my side, and I searched the horizon for something; what, I did not know.

"See?" His voice was joyful. A beautiful silver band stretched far out across the water. The shimmering light broke the expanse of gray extending from the sea to the sky.

"See?" he repeated.

I was so peaceful inside. Why had I never known this feeling before? For once, there was nowhere to go and nothing to do. Daniel and I stood together, unencumbered, simple, beautiful as the shore itself. The silver band grew wider and more luminous as it moved toward us. Mesmerized, caught in the warm breeze and the sensation of fullness, I watched the light. This must be a strange atmospheric condition of some kind. This thought was almost jarring—my social mind was trying to compartmentalize.

"That's so good, Karen!" Daniel rewarded my awareness with a shower of enthusiasm.

I was actually pleased with myself. I had recognized the intruder and stopped it in its tracks. My reward was a continuation of this blissful state of being.

"Just watch," he reminded me gently.

Indeed, there was something compelling to watch. The gray

sky moved back farther and farther as the band of light widened and approached the shore. The gulls in front of us suddenly stopped moving. They were suspended in midair, caught in some kind of magic.

"Daniel, what's going on?"

I noticed the waves had also stopped. Half crested, the white spray on top of the swelling waves was suspended. I looked quickly over at Daniel, whose face was radiant with joy. Light streamed from every pore of his little body. The band of light had almost reached us. If we didn't move, we would shortly be caught in it completely. I didn't know what that meant, I only knew I didn't want to run.

Daniel spoke so softly that his words floated in the wind like the gull feathers drifting across the sand. "Just stay right here, Karen. Not only with your body, but stay where you are right now in your heart."

How beautiful this place was, everything so delicately balanced, so rhythmically associated, each thing having its perfect place. And I was a part of it all. I had my place as well. For once, I was not an anxious consumer on the surface of the environment. I had an integral part—as important as, but not more important than, anything or anyone else. And suddenly I became aware of a low humming rising up around us. It seemed to be coming tenderly from everywhere. I looked down to find that each grain of sand had its own voice. Like a gigantic choir surrounding us, everything sang the same song. Tears rolled down my face. I sobbed for everything I had not known.

"Daniel, it's all alive, isn't it? My God, it's all alive! I never knew . . . why did I not know all this time it's all been alive?" Even as I cried, I was still full of love. My tears cleared away the debris in my heart and mind. And everything began to move in one majestic, integrated, harmonious swaying motion.

I felt my body join in, and for a few glorious seconds we all sang one song and danced one dance together. My arms grew feathers and became wings. My feet became hoofed and galloped across the beach. My hands turned in perfect spirals, and nautilus shells grew. All at once, I became everything that could be. And still the silver band continued its journey toward us.

"That's what happens when you're in your right mind. Isn't it beautiful?" Everything spoke at once, the words not coming only from Daniel this time. Simultaneously, I had said the same thing! Somehow, I knew to say the same thing. More important, somehow I knew the same thing. How?

Again, we all spoke at once. "That is the mind you were meant to have, the one that has been overshadowed by your social mind. The right mind can see the whole. It does not judge, it just watches everything with love. There is no need for competition for energy, for you have all you need. When nothing is separated, there is no lack. When you are not falsely isolated, there is no need to fear or worry."

"You mean, this is the way I could feel all the time?" I whispered, this time speaking alone.

"Of course," we all replied. "This is how you were meant to feel and be while you are on Earth."

Looking down, I was clearly in my own body again. But I was somehow illuminated from within. I looked like a paper lantern, soft light showing through my skin. Daniel stood at my side, entranced by the profoundly beautiful ribbon of silver, now just offshore. I could see shimmering particles of light moving within the band. I also thought I could see shapes beginning to form, almost out of the light itself. Faces and bodies softly emerged and disappeared again.

"Is there anyone in there, Daniel?"

"Look!" he replied enthusiastically. I concentrated harder on the ribbon of light. Out of an incandescent fog, people began to move outward and toward us. They were beautiful, like the men on the beach—strong, muscular, brown, and joyful. I was not afraid, but I was confused.

"Daniel, is that some sort of spacecraft?" I ventured. "Is that what this is all about? Are they visitors from another planet, coming to save us?"

Once again I heard rippling laughter, sent out with love, not judgment. "Oh, Karen, is it so hard to accept who you are?"

I sputtered, "But I am not like them . . . am I, Daniel? I mean, I don't seem to be . . . at least not until the last few minutes or so. What is that light? Where are they coming from? Who are they?" I continued to watch streams of joy in the form of human beings emerge out of the band.

"They're people, silly!" he said with a laugh. "They're Earth people who are in their right minds! Isn't that a funny phrase? You use it all the time, except you don't know what you mean when you say, 'He's not in his right mind.' See?"

"I'm sorry. I don't understand," I whispered. "They are so beautiful, Daniel, their bodies are transparent somehow. I can see light shining through them from somewhere inside."

"From you, too," he pointed out. Sure enough, my body continued to radiate light.

I tried to make sense of what he was saying. "How can you say they are Earth people? I saw them come out of that light. I saw that band move all the way from the horizon to here. I've never seen anything like that before, not even in Hawaii!"

"But we're not in Hawaii. "

"We're not in Hawaii?" I decided to sit down as these gorgeous beacons of light formed a circle of loving energy around me.

I was aware that my social mind had set up an enormous protest within me. It had started attacking Adam for energy. The argument was so familiar. "Get it together, Karen. It's time to stop all this nonsense and get concerned, worried, downright afraid. After all, look at what's happened to you today. Do you consider that normal? You've gone crazy. Just let me take care of you, Karen. Let's get away from this kid and all the other hallucinations and see if we can contact reality again. You have a practice to run, bills to pay, obligations. What are people going to think? You can't afford to go crazy."

"No!" I shouted. "No! You can't rob me anymore. You can't take my life away. I deserve to know who I am!"

Waves of joy swept over me. The energy of those surrounding me seemed to arc up even higher. Daniel beamed and patted my arm. "That's good, Karen. That's so good."

I felt incredibly strong in that moment. Every aspect of my being seemed to vibrate in recognition of my statement of liberation. I felt alive! I was filled with new courage, and I was ready to find out what I needed to know. "All right. We're not in Hawaii. Where are we, then?"

"In the Earth people's first home. Where else could we be?"

༺ TWENTY ༒

"Could you repeat that?" I said quietly. I had heard his words just fine, but I needed time to assimilate them.

Earth people's first home; what could that mean? Hadn't we always lived on this planet? I knew that some New Age people believed that we had actually come from Venus—at least I thought it was Venus. But that had struck me as strange. Why was it more probable that life had started on Venus?

"No, Karen," said the little boy, once again reading my mind. "I don't mean you came from another planet. At least not exactly. Well, most of you didn't. Anyway, what I meant was, this is the first place on Earth where people lived. You know, after Gaia built her body to help you, you all came to live here."

Gaia's body . . . Earth was not a giant piece of rock, but a being—a body that we were living on. My dream of the beautiful woman had been real! Gaia! I had to accept it. The experience I had on the beach was real, too. Everything was alive. It was all alive because Gaia was a sentient being with a living body.

I wanted him to confirm what I already knew. "Daniel, it's true, isn't it? Gaia is a living being and humans are supported by her, like a mother supports her babies!"

"Yep. Except babies usually treat their mothers a lot better than humans treat Gaia . . ." His words trailed off.

"So," I said, excited to know this part of my history, "this is the part of Gaia where we first landed, emerged, developed, what?"

He nodded his reply as I thought to ask an obvious question. "And where are we, by the way?"

"In the Pacific," he answered.

"I thought you said we weren't in Hawaii."

"Well, we kind of are, sort of, but . . ."

"Not exactly," I finished. "Tell me, please . . . where are we?"

"See, Hawaii and some other islands are what's left in your time of what's here now." My mind had caught on two of his words. "My time?"

"Well sure," he said. "You didn't think we were still in the twentieth century, did you? That's pretty silly. I told you that they . . ."

"Where . . . are . . . we?" I spoke very slowly, hoping to disengage the claws my social mind had on my understanding.

"Well, let's see," he mused. "How would you describe it? Can't really tell you in terms of centuries like you usually do, because . . ."

My need to know grew stronger than my patience. "Daniel, for God's sake, spit it out!"

"About seven hundred twenty thousand years before your time."

"We are seven hundred twenty thousand years from where I usually live?" I couldn't remember my geology classes . . . were there dinosaurs in this time?

"Of course there aren't!" Daniel said instantly. "They were much earlier."

"Why did you say Hawaii is what's left?" I asked, looking around us. "Are we on another island somewhere around Hawaii?"

"You could say that. It's a little bigger; well, maybe a lot bigger. Let's see, I'll measure it for you." There was a long pause while Daniel's eyes gazed off in the distance. "It's three thousand one hundred forty-three miles by seven thousand three hundred two miles. That's pretty big!"

"How in the world did you measure it? Are you telling me we're on a continent in the Pacific? A continent that's enormous, a continent that Hawaii is now a remnant of?"

"Yep," he said simply.

"Daniel, is this Atlantis?"

"Nope. They're just a colony. People from this place travel there."

"What did you say?" Asking people to repeat themselves is a really good way to buy enough time for your brain to catch up.

"Atlantis is in the Atlantic Ocean. This is the Pacific. Lots of Earth people go from here to there and to other places on Gaia as well. But you all started out right here. Didn't you ever wonder why you can find the same myths and symbols all over the world?"

"Carl Jung had a lot to say about that."

"Well, he made an easy thing awfully complicated," Daniel said. "He came up with this big mysterious theory about how all people share a single mind somehow and that's why they think up the same symbols. But you really do that because you all came from the same place. The same symbols all over the Earth isn't any different from Dutch people everywhere thinking about tulips and windmills. It's just part of where they came from."

I asked softly, "What do you call this place, Daniel?"

He smiled. "The people who live here don't have a name for it. They only have right minds, remember? No need to separate and categorize things."

"Are all the people on this continent like these people?" I looked out over the luminous group still surrounding me.

"Yep. They didn't start out that way. When they first got here, they were a real mess. But Gaia helped them and they grew great—not like your Earth people now."

"What do you mean?" I asked, bravely willing to have more of my intellectual debris swept away.

"Where you came from had gotten to be thick with awful density. That's why Gaia had to volunteer to get you out of there. Well, these guys took good advantage of their opportunity to drop the density and be on their way back home. But you just keep getting heavier and heavier. That's why Gaia is having such a hard time. She was never meant to carry the kind of weight people in your time keep piling on."

"Daniel, that's so horrible," I cried. "We are brutally damaging a living being! And it's the being who takes care of us. What's the matter with us?"

"You're lost." He looked deeply concerned. "You're all just awfully lost."

"You keep referring to us coming from somewhere else. Where?" Seeing his hesitation, I added, "Didn't you just say we didn't come from another planet?"

"Yep," he said. "Well, some of you came from other planets, but not the ones in your solar system. But most of you have only had bodies on Gaia."

Some of the people on Earth came from other planets. I decided I would ask about that later. Right now I was more interested in where I had come from, where the earlier people on Earth had come from. "What do you mean when you talk about how these people were when they first got here? Where were they in the first place?"

"Let's eat!" The little boy sprang suddenly to his feet and ran off, disappearing into the thick green underbrush. I looked around to find only deep, compassionate eyes gazing at me from all directions. One man reached out his hand, and I clasped it tightly. I was instantly infused with love. I still didn't understand where I was, but I wanted to stay here forever.

A large, bright yellow fruit was offered from someone else, and I gladly took it. Savoring the delicious, unfamiliar taste, I realized for the first time that it was a gift directly from Gaia. I stopped eating and closed my eyes for a moment. "Thank you, dear Gaia. Thank you for your gifts, for so long taken without gratitude. Thank you for never giving up, for standing firm underneath my feet, for allowing me to breathe and eat. Thank you for the clear water you send from the sky that sustains me and washes me clean. Thank you for volunteering to care for me . . ."

I felt deeply moved in that moment, realizing I had to thank this being for my very life. How do you do that? How do you thank someone who has given you life for thirty-eight years without ever being thanked?

I thought about how heartless human beings had been, carving great wounds across her body, burning down her forests, paving over her skin, making it impossible for her to breathe in the fumes made by our miserable machines.

"I am so sorry . . ." I whispered, hoping my words would find their way into her heart. "I apologize for all of us . . . I am so sorry." With that, I fell into her arms and, knowing I was indeed a child of the Earth, allowed myself to sleep.

✆ TWENTY-ONE ✇

"Hi." I heard a small voice somewhere off to my left. I had slept, but for how long?

"Hi." The little voice came again. I made what seemed like a monumental effort to open one eye. It was dark, and I was still on the beach. The waves were moving again. I could hear them breaking against the shore. Sitting up, I looked around and saw no one.

"Hi." This didn't sound like Daniel.

"I can't see you, whoever you are," I replied.

"Down here. Look down here." Attempting to locate the voice, I searched downward, but saw only obsidian sand in the black night.

"You have to use your abilities." Again, the apparently disembodied voice spoke. "That's the only way to see anything real."

"I don't have any abilities," I said sadly. "I'm beginning to realize that. My social mind . . . do you know what that is, whoever you are?"

"I know what it is."

"Well, my social mind kept me from realizing I had anything except it. I didn't know I had Adam, let alone abilities of any kind. I still don't know what they really are or how to use them. I'm not even sure who I am anymore." I had no idea who I was talking to, but somehow it felt safe. "Daniel, is that you?"

"No."

Hoping for further information, I waited in the silence for a moment before asking, "Who are you?"

"Use your abilities." The voice continued encouragingly. "You do have them, even when you don't realize it. All of Earth's people have them. That's the point, really."

"I don't know how," I answered, feeling a little sorry for myself.

I heard a gentle reply. "Where would you start to look?"

"I have no idea," I said without thinking.

"Sure you do, Karen. What have you been feeling since you've been here?"

That question was easy to answer. "A tremendous amount of love . . . some kind of tangible energy that these people just seem to give to each other and to me."

"Right." The voice sounded pleased. "And where do you feel that love the most?"

"Well, all over my body." That wasn't quite right. "In my heart the most."

"So . . ." it prompted in the darkness.

Excitedly I replied, "So look for my abilities in my heart!"

"That's right!" Softly it encouraged me. "Just like I said. Look down."

I lowered my eyes to my chest. Astonished, I saw a light in the darkness. Pulling the shirt away from my skin, I was able to look beyond its surface and straight into the center of my chest. But what I saw was not an anatomical heart at all. Instead there was a ball of beautiful, compelling light, turning slowly inside me. My heart seemed to be divided into sections by flexible membranes of light, slightly billowing, like sails in a gentle wind.

"What is that?" Filled with peace, I wasn't afraid to hear

the answer. There seemed to be no need to fear anything I might learn. I wanted what was mine to begin with.

"That's you," the voice responded. "That's the part of you that receives the energy from your soul and propels it throughout your being so you can live on Earth. That's the place where all the love comes in to sustain you while you're here. And, if you're willing to listen, that's where you can hear the voice of your soul."

"It's so beautiful." I could hardly believe this belonged to me. How could I deserve something so incredibly beautiful?

"Karen, you don't have to deserve it. It is you. It isn't something given as a reward for being good or accomplished in some way. It is you. That's what we have been trying to tell you. Pure love exists at the center of your being. And it's meant to flow freely throughout you."

I knew what was coming next. "I get it! I get it! Density! Density is what gets it all clogged up, right? Our social mind grabs all the energy and diverts it into judgments and segmenting and separating and developing opinions and all that stuff! We're supposed to be like the people here, with the energy of love running clear and smooth through our systems and out to one another. That's it! Isn't it?"

"That's so good!" Daniel had appeared out of the darkness. "Karen, that's so good!"

"Look, Daniel! Look at my heart!"

"I know. That's what I see in everybody all the time," he said, smiling. "You're all like that; you just forget when you get here and then it takes you forever to remember and then . . ."

"Daniel, who was talking to me?"

"You'll meet them a little later," he replied. "Right now, we have somewhere we need to go."

"Can I take this with me?" I said, concerned I might lose this newly discovered wonder within me. But I answered my own question. "Oh. Right. It is me. That's right. This is me! I can't leave it anywhere, can I?" I felt incredibly empowered. I wasn't that nasty, stealing, little woman after all. I had wondrous energy inside.

"Of course you can't lose it someplace, silly," he said. "Let's go. I want you to see something."

Dawn was beginning to break. Gorgeous, delicate pinks and lavenders pushed back the darkness. The scent of salt water and flowers wafted by on the warm breeze. As I walked behind this little boy, skipping in the early morning light, I knew I would follow him anywhere. Passion was finding its way to the surface from somewhere deep within me. I was filled with courage and a new kind of strength that came straight from my heart.

I had a right to know what had been hidden from me, from all of us. I wanted permanent freedom from that social mind. I wanted to take care of Adam. And I wanted to know about this soul that spoke to me. I had never heard it. Had it been talking to me all the time?

"Yep," Daniel called over his bare little shoulder. "Yep. It talks all the time."

"Daniel, am I ever going to be able to do that? You know, read other people's minds?" His capacity was still unnerving.

"Sure," he said simply. "But it's mostly just social mind chattering. It's better when you start listening to a person's heart. That's a completely different thing."

"Daniel, this soul . . . my soul talks to me all the time?"

"Yep," he said, continuing to walk down the beach.

"What does it say?" I knew his answer would not be simple.

He wasn't ready to tell me. "I think you should hear that for yourself."

"But I always thought the soul was somewhere else. I don't know, in heaven or somewhere."

"Nope." The sky was considerably brighter now, and the

sea had turned a clear blue, like Daniel's eyes. "That's just more misunderstanding. Your soul isn't far away at all. You're actually in the middle of it. Really, you have to work pretty hard not to hear it."

"In the middle of it?" What did that mean?

"Even when people know they have a soul, they've been trained to think it's really far away or that it's some kind of tiny spark in them. But that's not right at all."

He was right about that. When I had considered my soul, it had always seemed very distant, foreign somehow. "But what do you mean, I'm in the middle?"

"Well . . . well, just look!"

✎ TWENTY-TWO ✎

I didn't know where I was, but it didn't matter at all. Spectacular beauty surrounded me, and love was everywhere. This place seemed constructed of sheets of pure, incandescent light undulating across an endless plain. For all those miles there was nothing but love.

My heart was full, and my mind was gone. Somehow, even the concept of wondering where I was seemed strange. "Where" was irrelevant. Free from my mind, I was suddenly no one and everyone and this was somewhere and nowhere. I felt so full. I had struggled so long and hard to feel this way.

My heart turned, radiating the most wondrous light. It sent rays out in every direction, and light flowed through my body unchallenged and unstoppable. Bountiful light and love poured from a limitless source. And once I had received it, I could send it out for miles and miles. I could send it to every human being in the world, and I would still have enough. I would have more than enough to feed every living thing forever and ever.

And Gaia, dear beautiful woman—my love, my friend, my mother, my sister. I can give to you as well. I have enough to heal you—I can wash your wounds and erase your scars. I can hold your heart in my hands and calm it again. Trees and animals will spring forth whole again. Your oceans will become clean and clear. I can sweep the air with all this love, and all of your dear ones will breathe again. Come to me, sweet Gaia. Let me hold you up. Let me soothe you and stroke you, love you and care for you and all your children. I have more than enough.

"See?" Daniel's eyes found mine. "See . . . that's who you are."

Abruptly I flew backward at an amazing speed and found myself on the beach again. Daniel held my hands in his. I was overflowing with intense gratitude.

"My soul . . . that was my soul, wasn't it?" My voice was barely audible.

I could hear the same love in his words. "Yes, Karen. That's who you are. Your body exists in the midst of that vast field of energy. It's the body and mind that are tiny, not the soul."

Tears ran down my cheeks and I whispered, "That soul . . . that soul speaks to me constantly?" Seeing his nod, I continued, "And that soul pours energy into my heart?"

"Constantly." He gently wiped away my tears with his little hand.

"Daniel, what does it say? What does my soul want me to hear?" But he didn't need to answer, for I was already hearing the voice in my heart.

"Karen, you are loved by everything that is and can ever be. You are never alone. Just let go, allow me in. I cannot force my way in, nor would I wish to. But in exact proportion to the room you make, I will flow into every tiny space within you. I will fill you with everything you could ever need. Let go of the social mind, let go of your preoccupation with what it tells you. Everything is perfectly all right. There is no danger except that which you bring to yourself through density. Density serves only to separate us. Without me, you are isolated and cannot find what you need to sustain you. Let go of all that blocks me out. Come to me, Karen. Let go . . . let me flow into you and through you. Let me flow out into your world."

My heart blazed with a radiance rivaling the sun. Yet my

eyes did not hurt as I watched it. Glorious, pure light moved out from me in every direction. "Daniel, do you mean we've had it all backward? It's not that the soul is out there somewhere and we have to struggle to get to it? It's been right here all along? And it wants to come into us more and more, but we're clogged up with density and blocked by our social mind?" Overcome with gratitude, I stopped for a moment.

Gathering myself, I continued. "It's been there the whole time! I didn't know it was up to me to make room! I was always mad because the soul didn't just show up and do something to make my life better. All this time, my soul couldn't answer my prayers because I wasn't letting it come in! I thought it didn't work because prayers were just useless."

The realization that humanity had been so lost for so long was tremendously sad. We had been berating the cosmos for not saving us from our difficulties. We had been fearing some vengeful God, thinking we weren't good enough to be cared for. And all the time, our soul was right here! We were right in the midst of all of that love that was just waiting for us to make a little bit of room so it could flow in. And that powerful, punishing God . . . it was just our own construction, something our social mind had created with energy stolen from Adam! "We haven't been abandoned at all! Spirit isn't any farther away than it's ever been. We're just getting more and more difficult to communicate with!"

Daniel's eyes were full of compassion. "If you build up a thick social mind, and clog your body and your heart with density, how's your soul going to come in? It can't just blow through all that junk. That wouldn't be right, 'cause you always have to have free will. That's the way it is on Earth."

All of this made sense. We were trying so hard to get help from somewhere beyond ourselves. From my Christian friends who prayed for divine intervention, to those who sought peace from angels or crystals, we desperately wanted help out of the personal and cultural mess we were in. But Daniel was saying that without a real effort on our part to clear away the density within ourselves, the limitless love and help that surrounded us couldn't find room to get in!

We really didn't need to do the supplicating, the sacrificing, the religious rituals . . . the problem had nothing to do with persuading God that we were worthy of His attention. It was right there, always had been. "So, all of this pleading for outside help . . . God, angels and all of that, it doesn't fix anything, does it?"

"Nope," he said sadly. "As long as people hold onto the density they have, and continue to accumulate more, there will be no room for the soul to flow in."

We had been so far off track! The voice of the infinite wasn't ever going to boom from the sky, or appear as a choir of angels. It was much, much closer than that.

"Daniel," I cried. "I can receive the energy of my soul through my own heart, even hear what it has to say to me. But until now, I didn't even realize what my heart really was, let alone know to listen to it!"

"I know," he said quietly. "For some reason, Earth people worship that social mind. And that's about the worst thing they can do." Then, abruptly, he leaped to his feet and marched off down the beach.

I jumped up to follow him. "Where are we going? Daniel, where are we going?"

Glancing over his shoulder, he replied, "I want you to see something really important. Then you'll understand better, I think."

"Where, though?" I scrambled to keep up with him. "Where are we going?"

"I want you to see where human beings came from in the

first place." With that, he made a sharp left turn and headed toward the lush vegetation at the edge of the beach. He was well ahead of me when I saw him reach a thick cluster of palm trees and vanish among them.

◖◗ TWENTY-THREE ◖◗

All around me, rough, gray, slightly hairy trunks pointed straight to the sky like a herd of elephants flat on their backs. I rubbed the surface of the palm tree in front of me and wondered where Daniel had gone.

Remembering what my soul had said about never being alone, I decided I would be all right for a while without my little guide. I was constantly surrounded by love. I knew that now.

Walking peacefully among the trees, I thought about Gaia and the multitude of animals and plants she had created. Daniel had said once that she came from heaven. I wondered what that meant. If our souls didn't live in a far-off heaven somewhere, then what was heaven about? Why did Gaia come from there?

I could still hear the waves crashing into the beach, but it was good to be up off the sand. Here, the air was fragrant with life, and I remembered what it had been like to be inside the fern. Aware of much more than I had ever been before, I saw a thousand little green things pull sparkling light into themselves, each one reaching independently up toward the food of its being. It seemed they knew more than we did.

How did we get so lost? Certain things seemed obvious to me now. Gaia was the ground of our being, the source of our bodies, or vehicles, as Daniel called them. But the light of our soul was what created and sustained us.

"That social mind really isn't very smart, you know." A voice seemed to come from somewhere at my feet.

Looking down, I quickly asked, "Are you the one who was talking to me in the night?"

I already knew the answer. "You're the one I couldn't see! Come out this time. Please come out!" The ground under my feet was moist and the color of cinnamon. Turning around to see if there was someone behind me, I saw nothing but rich, green plants.

"Down here." Again, I looked down at my feet and saw nothing unusual. "Use your abilities. You can't see anything that's important if you just use your senses . . ."

I pondered the statement for a moment. "I'm supposed to look inside my heart. You told me that before! Thank you so much, whoever you are."

I concentrated on my heart, knowing about its capacity to radiate the light coming from my soul. I looked down after a moment, and the shimmering glow was there. As I thought about the intense love I had experienced, the ball of light began to turn and grow brighter. I filled up again with peace and wonderful energy.

"Now look."

In my blissful state, I looked down again. There at my feet was something I never in my wildest dreams thought I would see. "What? What in the world . . ."

"Hi," she said—at least it seemed like a she. As I struggled to understand what I was seeing, I lost focus on my heart. She disappeared.

"Use your abilities." I renewed my concentration, and there she was again . . . a small light fluttering around my right foot. Slightly larger than a butterfly, it generated a subtle array of beautiful pale colors. Now violet, then pink, peach, and gentle yellow, the light never stopped moving.

"What are you . . . who are you?" I fought to stay anchored in my heart. I could feel my social mind aroused and ready to steal energy. After all, this light was suspiciously like a fairy of some kind. Fairies were a myth, everybody knew that. With that thought, the light disappeared.

"Use your abilities."

"I know, I know." I was frustrated. "My social mind is so devious. If I lose my concentration for a second, bam! It's right there, ready to take over. Let me try again."

I thought about all the wondrous love I had been given, and knew I did not want to be trapped in my social mind ever again. But that wasn't going to be easy. I had lived a lot of years letting it get away with anything. From now on, life was going to be different. There was too much to lose.

When I was ready, I looked down again and there she was! Enormously pleased with myself, I searched the patch of light for gossamer wings. Why not? After everything I had learned, why not accept this as well? Nonchalantly I stated, "You're a fairy, right?"

"No," she replied.

"No?" I had been so ready to accept something I thought was impossible. "What are you, then?"

"A human being, just like you are," she said simply.

"What?" As quickly as I said it, I knew I was going to lose sight of the dazzling little light. I knew who had control of my energy in this moment.

"Get out of my way!" I commanded my social mind. And there the little light was again, now like an iridescent dragonfly by my left elbow.

"Well, not just like you are, but still . . . a human being," she said sweetly.

"But you don't seem to have a body!" I protested. "I mean, you look like just energy—no form, no vehicle, as Daniel would say. And you're so small! You don't seem anything like a human being."

I tried very hard to keep my heart completely open while I asked my questions. I knew I should simply accept what I was seeing, but I was so curious!

Flashes of ultraviolet blue sparkled among silver and pink light as the tiny being zipped past my face and stopped in mid-air, about four feet in front of me. "Well, it's just that I've had lots of time to develop and you haven't, that's all."

I had no sense that she was saying she was superior to me in some way as she continued. "We got here first. I'm from the first wave and you're from the second. We've just had more time."

"First wave? Like an ocean wave? I'm afraid I don't understand." Tiny, delicate bells were ringing somewhere. I realized it was her laughter.

"Well, I guess you could say it is like the waves of the sea. But, really, it's just that a group of us came to Earth first, and now another group is in the process of coming. You're with the second group."

"Oh. Okay," I mused. "Wait a minute! Came from where? Daniel told me Earth people did not come from anywhere else."

"I don't think he said that. Probably he said the only bodies you've ever had were on the Earth."

"You're right. He did put it that way." Now I had no idea what she had meant. "I'm really confused."

"Let me see if I can help. You know by now how unfortunate it is when a person thinks he is just a physical body."

I answered with passion. "It's a terrible mistake to think that way, or to think that you're just some kind of computer-mind, a linear, logical collector of information. That seems to be the way most people see themselves. Except for our emotions . . . we don't know what to do with them. We even regard them as the enemy when they get in the way of what we want to accomplish."

I tried to consider all I had learned. "Daniel said I have three spirits. I know about Adam and all the incredible work he did to create my body and keep it running. Is the second spirit the right mind?"

The tiny light darted back and forth for a moment. Her colors were so lovely, now like those in a drop of water in the sun.

"The second spirit is not the right mind itself, but it *is* what created that aspect within you. Just like your nature spirit created your physical body, the second spirit created your consciousness. I prefer to call it the natural mind, because I know your scientists have divided the physical brain into right and left hemispheres. This is different from that."

I nodded and waited for her to go on.

"The people on the beach showed you what a wonderful thing natural mind can be. It is simply consciousness, or awareness that you are a being and that you are living on Gaia. Unfortunately, the second wave has developed a social mind as well. Like your beautiful lakes and rivers have become polluted with awful things, your social mind has polluted your consciousness. The social mind eclipses the subtle natural mind."

Her colors dimmed a little as she said this. I was concerned. "Are you all right?"

"I am. It's just that I feel so distressed about Gaia." She paused and seemed to pull in more energy from somewhere. Suddenly blazing again with bright orange and red, she asked, "Now, what else would you like to know?"

"Well, let's see if I understand." I took in a deep breath. "The second spirit created my awareness of being alive and being on the Earth. That natural mind is what I could see in the people here. It was so wonderful, they seemed completely whole.

They didn't need to compete with each other, they were just being."

"That's right!" she said happily. "Natural mind gets everything it needs straight from the third spirit, the soul."

But I had a sobering thought. "Daniel told me how the social mind literally steals energy from other people. That's a pretty awful thing!"

"It does make for a lot of conflict and misunderstanding among you—and loneliness. When you are in your social mind, you are separated from your soul, from other human beings, from Gaia, and your relationship with Adam suffers tremendously."

What a mess we had made of our world. "I can see it would be different if we were all in our natural minds. But most people don't even know about it . . . I didn't! How can I be in my natural mind without getting run over by all those thieving social minds out there?"

How could I let my defenses down with such danger around me? But it was essential that I learn to do it. That was clear. So much of my contact with other people was about protecting myself, not losing ground, not being embarrassed or making a mistake. How could I just relax, especially now that I knew many of them had social minds who wanted to steal from me?

She was another mind-reader. "Karen, that's the beauty of it." Her colors calmed to silvery greens and blues. "When you are in your natural mind, other people's social minds cannot touch you. They cannot rob you of energy. In fact, when you are in your natural mind, you will find other people starting to move *out* of social mind. Often, without a single word, you can bring harmony into a situation. No one knows what happened, but everyone feels better. Then there is more room to creatively solve your problems. But you know what?"

"What?"

As though whispering a secret, she said, "Many of the problems that seem so real, and so terribly important, dissolve once you enter your natural mind."

"Wait a minute." I couldn't believe it could be that easy. "You aren't talking about glossing over problems, pretending they're not important. I don't know if I really understand. The natural mind has a particular kind of energy that comes in from the soul. The social mind has another kind of energy, which it must obtain by stealing from other people?"

"That's right," she said.

"When we're in our social mind, no matter what the interaction with another person may seem to be, what's really going on is that two social minds are battling for power."

"Right."

"And the only outcome of that kind of interaction is that someone wins and someone loses. That's why we struggle so hard with one another. The energy of our own social mind is dependent on winning competitions with other social minds!"

"Pretty sad, isn't it?" she said.

"It's tragic," I cried. "We have so many problems with other people because we live in the part of ourselves that does nothing but try to knock the other guy down so it can be stronger."

"When you go into your natural mind, the competition stops. Problems begin to dissolve because the other person's social mind can't steal from you. Your own social mind can't steal from the other person because you deactivate its abilities when you move into your natural mind."

My heart was pounding. "And that takes care of a lot of problems that seemed so real when they were fueled by the desperate competition for energy!"

"That's right," she said merrily. "And the remaining problems are solved more easily by cooperation between natural minds, instead of competition between social minds."

"So the solutions to our conflicts have been within reach all along!"

"Right inside you!" She darted back and forth in front of me like an ecstatic butterfly. "Isn't that wonderful?"

I was getting dizzy watching her. "Can you slow down a little? I need to understand how to do it. How does a person get into his or her natural mind?"

"Oh, Karen, you already know the answer!" She stopped near my ear. I could hear a steady vibration, almost a humming sound, and then she whispered, "Look in your heart."

"Okay, okay, I'm slow. I admit it." I was exasperated with myself. How many times did I have to hear something?

"You aren't meant to be slow, you know," she said with compassion.

"I'm usually quite intelligent. I grasp new information very well, but this . . ."

"This isn't about collecting information," she said quietly.

"No . . . no, it's about discovering who I was meant to be, isn't it?" I had been terribly confused about that for a very long time.

"Yes, it is, and you were never meant to be slow."

"What do you mean?"

"Well, you were meant to be fast, like me!" She sped back and forth, a dazzling display of light and movement, every color of the spectrum sparkling in an endless display of beauty.

"I can't do that!" I exclaimed, watching her glorious ability.

She laughed. "Not right now, but this is what you were meant to be. Karen, you are pure, quickly vibrating energy encumbered by ponderous density. Your social mind is composed of tremendously slow energy, and it's filled with even thicker energies that you collect, really steal, from other people. Anything of truth you try to run through that system is going to get stuck and never be seen again. That's why it takes human beings so long to understand who they are. I told you before, you can't see anything real as long as you just use your senses."

I needed some hope. "But the natural mind can understand truth, right?"

"Of course. The natural mind was meant to provide an open channel from the soul directly to Adam and the person in his or her lifetime on Earth. But the second wave took a terrible turn and developed the social mind, which isn't connected to anything at all except things on the outside. That's why you are all so desperate. You're starving to death."

My heart was sinking. "What do you mean?"

"Well, you have to get what you need from outside yourself because you're disconnected from the source of all energy, the source of your being." Her voice was filled with sadness. "When people start to run out of food, they panic. They do all sorts of things to ensure their survival."

I knew there was something else we could do. "The natural mind can get all the energy we need!"

"That's right. Karen, just look down again."

I did as I was told, and found myself staring again at the beauty contained within my chest. There it was, the magnificent ball of shimmering light.

"What makes that center turn, Karen?" she asked.

I answered quickly. "Those walls inside the ball."

"No," she said patiently. "They facilitate the movement. But like a water wheel, something must push against those walls to cause them to turn."

Again, I looked down at the splendor within me. Tiny spheres of rose- and gold-colored light danced inside each chamber. "I can see lots of moving light in there. Actually, it looks like particles of light pouring in from somewhere."

"Where do you suppose it's coming from?" she asked, with a touch of amusement in her voice.

I suddenly realized. "It's the tangible energy that comes right into me from the soul! You told me to look in my heart to get to my natural mind. Is this my natural mind? Is that what you are telling me?"

"It's an essential part of it."

"This energy is meant to fuel my life, isn't it?" I said excitedly. "My heart should work just like that water wheel, and I'm supposed to keep it open and unclogged, so the energy can get where it needs to go. And I need to stand right next to that wheel so I can feel that wonderful, pure, energy coming in! That's my natural mind—me standing next to that water wheel."

I felt gloriously free in this moment. I had found the fountain of life, and it was right inside me! "This is wonderful! I'm so beautiful! Look, just look!"

Radiant beams of light shone from my heart, and the little voice began to laugh like a thousand tiny wind chimes. "You are beautiful! That's what we've been trying to tell you! Karen, you are beauty itself." Her light spun around mine, and I was filled with love beyond my greatest imagination.

"More, Karen. Come on! You can do it!" Her voice was exhilarated, delighted, filled with love. "Let more come through. It's all there waiting for you to open the way! It's all there for you. Let it in, make the room, let yourself be what you were meant to be!"

I felt like I could do anything. I simply let go and opened my heart as wide as I could. Like a mighty waterfall, energy poured into my heart, sparkling, radiant, strong. It spun the wheel faster and faster. I was delirious with joy, opening myself even wider. My body and mind seemed to disappear in the torrent of beauty. I was pure jubilation—clear, unencumbered, and free!

The humming sound came again, and I knew this time it

was Gaia herself. And I looked to see her beside me, spectacular heart center running smooth and fast, tremendous power and love propelling life forward, filling each creature and plant. We spun together, waterfalls of light and glory, and sang the song of Earth.

I did not care if I ever found "Karen" again.

✄ TWENTY-FOUR ✄

"The thing is, you have to know who you really are and stay on the Earth at the same time! I know that's hard. That's why people who get out of their social minds often end up being called crazy. The other social minds don't like it when somebody starts telling people what's outside their little world. You know how they are, scared of getting ended. That's how they fight back."

That's Daniel, I thought. The last I could remember, I was in an enormous dance of love with Gaia. Now I was lying face down on the ground, my head on my arm. The earth was fragrant and warm. I opened my eyes and looked up. I could see his short legs in front of me. My eyes went higher to see the red swimming trunks, little pot belly, and familiar smiling face.

"Daniel! Where have you been? I had the most wonderful experience!" I was so happy to see him. Looking around, it appeared we were still somewhere in Hawaii.

"We're not in Hawaii."

"I know. I know. But it's close enough. I mean, we haven't gone somewhere completely different from where we met the men on the beach, and where I was talking to that . . . that little light?" I struggled to sit up.

"Nope," he said, and he began to walk away.

"Wait a minute!" I cried, climbing to my feet. "Wait. Where are we going?"

"Come this way. I'll show you!" I had heard that phrase so many times today. Was it still today? Had my airplane landed a long time ago without me on board? Had they launched a frantic search for the woman who had mysteriously disappeared somewhere in the air between Boise and Seattle? Whether it was still today or not really didn't matter. I was never going to be the same again, that was clear. And off we went, deep into the jungle.

Pushing back giant, deep green leaves hanging out over the narrow path, I followed behind my small friend. The air had a sense of mystery here, as the overhanging botanical majesty began to diminish the sun. Birds were everywhere—now bright yellow, then a flash of red or blue.

Hoping to see my new, color-flashing friend, I looked deep into the greenery. Here and there I thought I saw a bit of sparkling light, but it was gone in the blink of an eye. I thought about my conversation with her and wondered where she was . . . what she was. "A human being of the first wave," she had said. I wanted to know more.

"Daniel, where do human beings come from?" I was struck by the irony. Shouldn't the seven-year-old be asking the adult where people come from? I hoped his explanation would be as simple as an anatomy lesson, but I knew it wouldn't.

"From the unity, of course," he replied. Without even a pause, he continued to march down the path.

As I studied his small back and steady pace, I tried to understand what he had said. "The unity?"

Without turning around he answered. "Where all the souls are one . . . no separation, no density, nothing but pure love. That's where you all came from in the first place. But gosh, that was an awfully long time ago!"

"You mean heaven? Humans' souls live in heaven until we are born, then we live on the Earth. And when we die, we go back to heaven, right?" That was basically what I had thought in the middle of sleepless nights.

"Nope." We had come to a small clearing, and Daniel stopped to look up at me. "Gaia came from heaven, but I'm afraid the souls of human beings left there a long time ago. Like I keep telling you, you got lost . . . really, really lost."

It seemed like a good idea to sit down. I found a patch of spongy moss and intently watched Daniel to see if he was going to offer more information. But he had gotten diverted by a gorgeous crimson hibiscus blossom. Stroking it carefully, he murmured, "Gaia, you make the most beautiful things."

"Daniel," I called. "Can you talk to me about this? Please don't leave me hanging now! Gaia is a being, not a rock. I sure know that now. But are you telling me there are different kinds of souls or something?"

"Well, kind of, sort of, not exactly." He came and sat down next to me. "The souls of all the human beings and Gaia used to live together in the unity. But then something so incredibly horrible happened, nobody has gotten over it, and it's been millions of years!"

⟅ TWENTY-FIVE ⟆

"What?" I blurted, not sure I could handle the answer.

"Yep. That's how long human beings have been lost."

"Are you telling me we got lost from heaven somehow?" I said, my heart beginning a familiar polka in my chest. "Are you saying we haven't been there for millions of years? Daniel, how could that be?" This was the most shocking thing I had learned all day. How could we have gotten lost from heaven?

"Well, all souls have free will, even in the unity," he began matter-of-factly. "And a long time ago, some souls decided to use that free will to go in a different direction from the rest. They didn't mean to do anything harmful, they just wanted to go a different way. So they did, and it caused an awful mess. We're still trying to get everybody to come home." Very earnestly, he looked across at me. "Any other questions?"

"Any other questions!" I cried. "Daniel, are you kidding? Where did all of these souls go? Why can't they just go back with the others if that's what everybody wants?" Unconsciously, I had leaped to my feet. "Lost from heaven—that's horrible!"

"We have tried so hard to bring you all home. But once you developed social minds, you could hardly hear us at all. How could we bring you home if you couldn't hear us?" He gazed up at me, waiting for an answer that I could not provide.

I was suddenly horrified. "Daniel, oh my God, are you saying that story in the Bible about Lucifer and the fall from heaven is true? Are we those souls who went with the devil?"

"It's all right, Karen," he said, reaching out to pat my leg. "That's just another one of those misunderstandings. You didn't go with any devil and you weren't cast out of heaven. It's just you all took action that hurt everyone. You didn't mean to cause harm."

Feeling frantic, I asked, "Where are the souls of human beings if they aren't in heaven?" Were we just floating around out there somewhere, hopelessly lost forever?

"Well, over millions of years, the souls forgot a lot about who they were and where they came from." He watched me for a moment to see if I could handle any more. Apparently deciding there was a little room, he continued, "They started getting a lot of density. They stayed together in a, well, a kind of . . . well, they stayed together in a chunk."

"A chunk! Daniel, are you saying the souls of human beings aren't in heaven, they're in some kind of lost chunk?"

He stood and looked at me with enormous compassion.

I choked out my question. "What's going to happen to us? How can we ever get home?"

To my surprise, his answer sounded cheerful. "That's why Gaia decided to come in the first place—to give the lost souls a place to have lifetimes so they could remember who they were. Then they could drop their density and return home! That's why she came. Isn't that wonderful?"

"Well, yes. But I don't think we're getting it!" I felt desperate about our predicament. "With all I've learned today, it seems like we're getting more density, not less. We can't even hear our own souls anymore."

Tears began to fall as I realized what had resulted from our confusion. My new heart seemed unable to bear the pain. "Gaia . . . Gaia, my God, we're killing her."

"Well," he said gently, "that's why we decided to show somebody . . . that's you! Like I told you, every time a teacher comes to Earth, a few people listen, but then their social minds come in and tell them not to believe anything they can't measure, and that's the end of it." His eyes clouded and he muttered, "Or the human beings kill him."

"Like Jesus . . ." I knew what he meant. After all, I had lived through the assassinations of President Kennedy and Martin Luther King. I knew about Mahatma Gandhi, Tibetan monks, Christian martyrs. It was true, the peacemakers and the revolutionaries of the heart were attacked mercilessly. First they were discredited, then they were threatened and finally they were murdered. "So our very souls are encumbered by density? I thought we could count on that soul to give us love—the energy through the wheel."

"You can, Karen," he said brightly. "Even though the souls are weighed down by heavy energy, they are still much lighter than human beings on the Earth. Even as they are, they are still much closer to the energies of love."

"Why do they need us, Daniel? Why do we exist at all?" Somewhere along the line, I had started pacing. I stopped and looked at the little boy for a solution to this age-old question.

His face softened. "You're very, very important. You are supposed to be a kind of servant to your soul. You are sent here to gather particular information, certain lessons for the soul. That's how it makes progress."

"I'm supposed to help my soul? I didn't know it needed anything. I thought it was perfect!" This was a revolutionary idea. I had always thought my soul would help me, if I could just contact it somehow. It had never occurred to me that I might be of some use to it.

"Yep," he nodded. "You can help a lot. And your soul is perfect. It just needs to be freed. That's where you come in, thanks to Gaia. She saw you lost out there and couldn't stand it. So she opened a kind of school. Human beings can come to gather information their souls need. But when your social minds developed, you quit listening to your souls and kind of went off on your own way."

"So we don't get the job done and the soul has to send out another personality in another body?" This was a tragedy. This went way beyond Moses getting exiled to the desert for forty years.

"Yep," he replied, shrugging his shoulders. "Over and over and over again."

"I guess reincarnation is real, after all." That sure stuck in my throat. I didn't want to believe the years of stories people had been boring me with about their dramatic past-life experiences.

"Yep. Well, kind of. People get awfully interested in what they were doing in past lifetimes, but it really doesn't matter. Your lifetime is like a coat the soul wears, a temporary covering. Studying past lives is like devoting time to looking at all the coats you've owned in your life."

I understood. "So, if personalities and bodies are just temporary coverings, but we forget and go our own way, it's like if a coat were to walk out of my closet and take off on its own!"

Daniel was giggling. "Pretty funny. Especially if the coat thought it was real, and you weren't, and wouldn't listen to you. And what if it got really cold, and you needed that coat, and it wouldn't come back?"

"Like the soul needs us to use this lifetime to gather what it needs to go home?" I didn't think this was so funny. We had been lost for a long time. We needed to get our act together and quit fooling around.

There were leftover pieces to my puzzle. "But Daniel, that little non-fairy person, she said she was human . . . the first wave

. . . she was so different. These first and second waves; what's that all about?"

"It's just that there were so many lost souls, Gaia asked that they be given lifetimes in two groups, so that she wouldn't be overwhelmed. You were talking to one of the human beings who came into physical form with the first group." Looking away for a moment, he added, "I'm afraid they did a lot better with their opportunity than you guys are doing."

Sadly, I had no evidence to the contrary. But an interesting thought occurred to me. I had thought the little light-being was a fairy. Maybe that was the answer to the legends about fairies and little people all over the world. Maybe they were humans of the first wave!

Daniel grinned. "Yep, those legends are true, Karen!"

I would never get used to his reading my mind. "Daniel, I do wish you wouldn't do that! How can I keep anything private from you?"

"Can't," he replied simply. "I can hear everybody all the time anyway, all over the Earth. You all mostly sound the same, I'm afraid. Lots of worries and fears, not much love."

"But what we call fairies are real after all?" I smiled at the idea.

"Yep. Well, kind of. They don't have wings and all that stuff. But, some of them occupied the Earth at the same time as the second-wave people."

After all I had been through today, the fact that these incredible, magical beings really did exist came as a wonderful surprise. "So, the little people—the Irish leprechauns, the menehunes my friend talks about, the trolls of the Germans, the elves of the Dutch—those were first-wave beings, too?"

"Well, the stories about them are all mixed up. But they did really live on the Earth." He said the next words with a great deal of sadness. "See, the more you poison Gaia, the fewer first-wave beings there are. They leave because they can't breathe in the middle of all the density."

We were so terribly lost, we had sent a lot of the magic out of our world. Why were we so different? "Why was the first-wave group so successful, Daniel, and we're having such a hard time?"

"Partly because you spent a much longer time in the chunk. And partly it's just a result of free will. People can always make the choice to set down density or pick up some more. Unfortunately, once a lot of people start to pick it up, they teach others to do the same. Before you know it, everybody's lost. Besides, the first wave never developed a social mind. Isn't that the most beautiful creature?"

He scrambled off after an iridescent blue butterfly.

A protest died at my lips, and I decided to follow him. We let the innocent daughter of Gaia lead us where she would. We ran back and forth, eyes heavenward, following this bit of color on the wind. Drifting out of sight like a dream, she pulled us well away from the path, then disappeared completely.

᥍ TWENTY-SIX ᥏

I looked around, unable to find any sense of direction. Giant ferns, wrapped by enormous vines, surrounded me and the canopy above was so thick, I couldn't see the sky. It began to rain. Warm water showered down over my body. Lifting my face, I let myself be cleansed before returning to my concern about where I was.

"Daniel, where are we?" Somehow, I knew he was not going to be there. I wondered why he insisted on doing this, only half anxiously. Pulling fragrant red berries from one of the vines, I decided there were far worse places to be stranded. The luscious, sweet fruit filled my senses as I looked into the seemingly impassable greenery. With a measure of relief, I considered that this time Daniel had disappeared without anything strange happening. I decided to just sit down and relax for a while.

This was a wonderfully beautiful place. I wished that I knew more about these spectacular plants. The tip of a lush leaf brushed my arm. I was amazed to see that it was actually bigger than my torso. That butterfly really had led us deep into the jungle. Here, things have had a chance to grow undisturbed for a very long time. I stroked the stem of an odd, bright green, slightly hairy plant. Seeing how very delicate it was, I wondered how far away I was from the ocean. Maybe Daniel was just giving me an opportunity to rest. I certainly deserved it. I stretched my legs out and reached for some more fruit, comfortable to have nothing to do for a while.

How was I ever going to get home? I smiled a little with the realization that term now had two meanings. I did want to get home to my family and friends, but I had a new desire. I wanted to go home to "the unity," as Daniel had called it. And to be perfectly honest about it, I wanted more of the intensely moving experiences I had been having recently.

My fingers ran lightly over the grass by my side, and I remembered to thank Gaia, just as Daniel had done. She really did make magnificent things. I wondered about the theories of evolution. Certainly man did not develop from the apes, as I had learned in school. Daniel had told me very advanced human beings were running around on the planet a very long time ago. And what about plants? Did Gaia just randomly create what she wished? Did science really know anything about it?

Suddenly, I heard sounds in the jungle. Far away, they still seemed very loud. What could make such a noise? I jumped to my feet as they became closer. It seemed the Earth itself was shaking. There was a horrible sound of trees falling, and I could see giant ferns being smashed. The Earth was moving under a tremendous force. I placed my feet far apart for balance and frantically looked for a place to run. It must be something like a bulldozer. Adrenaline was coursing through my body. Wait a minute, they didn't have machines like that seven hundred twenty thousand years ago. What the hell was going on?

A moment ago, everything had been in perfect balance, now magnificent living things were being pulverized, ground into the earth. Green liquid oozed out of the formerly impeccable plants, and the red berries ran like blood over my feet. Terrified about my own safety, I was astounded at the destruction of the beauty around me. How could this happen? Damn developers don't have a clue about the environment, I thought as I searched for higher ground. I'm going to let them know they could have killed somebody out here.

The sound had become a roar, I couldn't find anywhere safe. I'm going to have to just stand here and hope they see me. Pulling myself up to my greatest height, I was fueled with a righteous anger, determined to make my opinion known. Bulldozers in paradise—couldn't human beings leave anything alone?

An immense noise rumbled directly over my head. What was left of the green life around me withered as the sounds reverberated above me. What could it be? I put my hands over my ears and searched the sky. A man's face loomed ten stories above me,

My knees gave way, and I crumpled to the ground, which shook violently as this giant began to move. His feet! Oh, my God, where were his feet? I looked around desperately. If he stepped on me, I would be dead in an instant!

There was a sudden movement of air, like wind being sucked out of a building in a fire. I knew I was directly in line with the monster's boot. It was all over. There was nothing I could do. Just as the plants all around me were now unrecognizable, I was going to be crushed.

"Use your abilities." The voice seemed to speak inside my head.

"I don't know how!" I cried out. "Help me, I don't know how!"

From somewhere deep within I heard, "You know where to go. Use your abilities." But the thunderous roar of the giant continued, and his foot swept down toward me like a wrecking ball. Tensing my body and my mind, I prepared for death.

Calmly, the voice said, "Let go, Karen. Don't constrict. Open, release, let go of it all."

"Open?" I protested violently. "Open, now? I can't, I can't!"

As the foot blocked out the light, I cried, "Help me! Please, help me!" Taking one last, deep breath, I closed my eyes and braced myself for tremendous pain.

"Oh, Karen, that won't work!" This was a different voice. The roaring had stopped, and I opened my eyes. There was a familiar but disappointed little face. "You really do have to start paying attention, or you're going to stay lost for another million years!"

"Pay attention?" My voice sounded like bending metal, and my body trembled uncontrollably. Frantically, I looked around for the foot, the giant, and the jungle, but could not see them.

In fact, we did not seem to be anywhere at all. A sparkling profusion of silver, pink, and pale lavender light drifted all around us, and a sense of profound serenity surrounded me on all sides. Somewhere in the distance, tiny bells rang. I managed to squeak out a question. "Am I dead?"

"Of course not, silly! You still have the same vehicle to use. But, Karen, I thought you had learned more than that."

Fear continued to crash through me as I scanned my environment for danger. "What happened? Who was that man?"

"Just a regular human being walking around."

The adrenaline in my body found a worthy cause and I exploded. "What does that mean? Daniel, I could have been killed! Don't you care about my feelings? I was scared out of my mind! Just a regular human being? He was a hundred feet tall!"

"Eighty-six feet." The child looked at me solemnly.

"What?" I was filled with righteous anger. "Who cares whether it was a hundred feet or eighty-six feet? I almost died out there!"

"Actually," Daniel said matter-of-factly, "he was just a normal person. It was you who had changed. You were very small, and he was, like I said, just a regular human being walking around."

How could he continue to torture me? "Daniel, that can't be true! He was so destructive. Trees were falling, plants were dying everywhere. It was terrible, didn't you see that?"

"That's what I'm trying to tell you, Karen. One human being, filled with density, can be a very heavy and destructive force."

"You mean that's what one person does to the environment when he simply walks through it?"

He nodded.

I could hardly believe it. "My God, one person has that effect, even without a bulldozer? I thought the end of the world was here."

"That's how it feels to everyone when a second-wave human being shows up. Pretty sad, huh?"

I searched for a little hope. "Are we all like that?"

"Nope," he said with a faint smile. "He was one with a lot of density. Some of you are much lighter."

I shook my head. "We must have switched time zones somewhere along the way. He wasn't at all like those guys on the beach, or the little light I was talking to."

"Yep," he said. "Moved back to the time where you guys live. Quite a difference, huh?"

"An awful difference," I groaned.

"Like I said, the first wave of human beings really took better advantage of the opportunity Gaia offered. I guess you've seen firsthand now what the difference feels like to her. She was never meant to support the kind of energy that you just experienced. And now there are so many of you just like that or even worse!"

"Why, Daniel? Why are we getting heavier and heavier, as you put it? What's the matter with us?"

"Well, souls are continuing to arrive from the chunk. That means there are lots of people on Earth who are in their very first lifetime after eons being lost. I'm afraid they bring a lot of heaviness with them. After all, they haven't had any opportunity at all yet to get cleansed of all the density they accumulated."

I thought for a moment. "Are you saying that the increase in violence on the Earth in recent years has to do with some kind of difference in the type of souls who are coming into bodies? It's not all sociopolitical stuff?"

"No. But social minds develop around those denser souls and then you get the so . . . soci . . . soci . . . what you said." Abruptly, he started a child's dance of some sort. Whirling and turning, arms outstretched, he ran past me, light cascading off his arms like water from a heron's wings. As he continued to move away from me, I had no choice but to follow him.

This was a wondrous place . . . the air was filled with a magical electricity. Light flowed over the surface of my skin, like the water in my shower. Loping behind the little boy, I stretched my arms out and watched the particles of silver and pink bounce from the surface of my hands and spray over my forearms like the surf hitting the rocks on the seashore.

Shooting through the waves of energy, my chest broke through sheets of windowed light, cutting its way and splitting the endless sea of silver. Light shot up into the air like sparks from a campfire on a summer night's beach, and drifting back downward, they swirled a spiral dance of magnificent intensity; now gold, now red and blue, silver and orange. Purple fire landed in my heart and exploded, sending volumes of tiny spheres of light out around me to multiply ten thousandfold.

"Daniel . . . this is so beautiful. Look! Look what I can do!" I was overflowing with elation. A deep, rich joy filled my every corner. The boy turned and watched as I managed to catch another spark with my heart and burst again into a majestic fountain of exhilarating light.

"Karen, that's so good!" The little voice was delighted, and I continued to play in the light like a child on the seashore, throwing armfuls of refracting color high into the air and laughing from deep inside my being as it showered back over me.

Splashing happily in the endless supply of energy, I suddenly caught a glimpse of something. Startled, I stopped and turned to view the awful spectacle in front of me.

‿❧ TWENTY-SEVEN ❧‿

I could see her well ahead of me. Dazed, I began to approach in disbelief, then stopped about fifteen yards away. Filled with dread, I spoke quietly to Daniel. "Tell me what's going on . . . please just tell me . . . what . . . how can this be?"

"We just want you to watch for a little while, Karen. Just watch." His words were achingly compassionate, and I did as I was told.

My heart was breaking, but I kept my eyes on this woman in a bubble. She appeared to be struggling fiercely, pounding with her fists, yelling, pacing back and forth, agitated, afraid. In the midst of the spectacular field of light, she was cut off by walls of a different kind of energy. Cloudy and speckled with black and brown, this prison seemed much too small for her.

Again and again she marched across the tiny space, flailing and crashing against its walls, sometimes falling to the floor in despair. I was desperate to help her. There was so much incredible beauty surrounding her, but she didn't seem to be able to see it. Caught like a prisoner in an interrogation room, this woman could not see beyond her one-way glass.

To my horror, the woman suddenly began punching her stomach, legs, and arms. As I watched her, muffled sentences began to reach my ears, and I was appalled to hear the blasts of terrible condemnation she fired at herself.

My own agitation increased beyond my ability to contain

it. "Daniel, for God's sake, what's she doing in there? We can't just stand out here—we have to help her!"

"Just watch, Karen." There was an urgent sound in the child's voice.

The woman suddenly sat down. Holding her head in her hands, she did not move for a long time. Then, standing up again, she began to pace and push on the walls. The bubble had grown more pockmarked with dull brown and black spots. It seemed that the more the woman struggled, the more opaque the walls became. Soon, we would have no view of her at all.

"All right, Karen. It's time to go closer. She can't see you. Just go up as close as you need to. I want you to look into her face." Again, the little boy's words were tremendously compassionate. Good, I thought, at least he cares as much about this woman as I do. We'll be able to do something for her.

Like the bug-splattered windshield of a car after a long trip, the walls of the bubble were increasingly covered with debris. I crossed the remaining distance between us, put my face up against the bubble, peered inside, and promptly fell backward in shock.

"Daniel. Good God!" I cried, struggling back up on my feet. I felt compelled to look again, nausea rising in my throat at the sight inside. The woman continued to struggle, tears rolling down her face. But that face . . . that face was mine!

"It is all right, Karen." A quiet voice spoke beside me. "I know it is hard to look, but I am right here." Looking quickly around, I couldn't see anyone. The voice didn't sound like Daniel's.

"It's me . . . my God, that woman trapped in that bubble is me." Sobs broke my words, and I couldn't continue for a moment. The bubble continued to be splattered with the dark substance, and I could barely see the woman. She had sat down again, apparently exhausted.

"How can it be? I'm here, I'm right here. But that's me over there, isn't it? It's not somebody who looks like me, it is me." I didn't know whether to attend to my collapsing mind or my breaking heart. I felt enormous compassion for the human being who was suffering so intensely. Still, my mind couldn't accept that I could be in two places at once. "What . . . what am I doing in that bubble? How did I get there?"

"You built it for yourself, Karen." The soft voice spoke again—kind, not blaming.

"I built it? I have no idea what you're talking about. How could I have built something I don't even recognize? And how could I be here and there at the same time?"

"Most human beings build one for themselves." I could barely see myself inside the bubble, now thickly covered with the dark material.

"What is it? Why would people build such an awful thing?" There was no movement in the bubble at all. Now I must be lying down again.

"It begins to happen the day you are born. You are not welcomed as a great soul, but as a nothing that must be built up into a something."

I still had no idea who this voice belonged to. "Daniel was telling me about that a while ago, but what does that have to do with this bubble?"

Ever so gently, my instructor continued. "If you are cut off from knowledge of your own being, you become lost and afraid. Those around you have long forgotten the truth of their being as well. Without this awareness, human beings become vulnerable and frightened. They begin to create protection for themselves, and in doing so, they create a wall between what they think of as 'me' and what in truth is 'I.'"

"I'm sorry. You've lost me."

Patiently, the voice explained, "You see, out of ignorance

and fear, each of you becomes a hardened capsule within the enormous field of the soul. The energies and wisdom of the soul continue to surround you, but you cannot see them or feel them."

"Wait a minute! Are you saying that we are standing in the middle of my soul right now, and that's me, stuck in some kind of capsule over there?"

"Yes, that is right."

"And I created that capsule myself, out of fear and ignorance about the reality of who I truly am?" I had no idea whom I was talking to, but that didn't seem as important as rescuing myself from that polluted prison.

"Very good, Karen." The voice sounded pleased. "Your awareness has been captured inside the walls of your body, and inside the walls of your senses. The reality that you worship is only a reality created by the limited information that comes through those senses. But that is only a part of reality, a tiny layer in a greater multilayered existence. For centuries people of science have asked what people saw or heard, what they tasted or felt. They only believe in what can be known through the senses."

"But what's all over the inside of the bubble, the capsule?" I had an idea.

"What do you think, Karen?" All day long, no one had been willing to just give me a simple answer.

I looked again at the awful, mottled mess. "Well, I think it must be density. It looks so thick, very different from the rest of the energy I've been seeing. It just feels heavy." The more I talked, the more sure I was of my answer.

"That is very good." The voice reflected genuine pleasure at my understanding.

I was concerned about the other me. "Why am I so upset in there? I mean, it does look like a very small space to have to live in, but she's—I'm—really actively distressed . . . at least I was. I haven't seen any movement for a while, I guess she's—I've—calmed down."

"Most personality selves are agitated and afraid. They attack themselves with words and self-destructive behavior. As you have seen, the more they do that, the more density is created. But often, those who become most agitated are like you."

"How am I different?"

"You have been trying for a long time to get out. The personality self who knows in her heart that she is separated from her soul begins to struggle against her confinement. Unfortunately, often she goes about it in the wrong way."

"I don't understand."

The voice spoke slowly, "Trying to reach spirit by running frantically from place to place, searching desperately for a teacher or technique, a church, a group, or a cause only results in the loss of valuable energy. The answer is always inward."

I thought about how human beings would try anything to put meaning in their lives. Sometimes they came up with some pretty strange methods. But the whole time, the answer had been in the last place we would look.

I wondered what could come of all that running around. "If nothing is accomplished by looking to the outside, then what?"

"The personality becomes more afraid, and makes a thicker capsule around itself. Without a connection to the soul, it flounders in confusion, loneliness, and despair. It is only a very tiny thing, with a lot of whistles and bells, making a lot of noise in its world. It knows deep inside that it is not the whole of your being. Its little kingdom in the capsule is only an illusion. Knowing this, it constricts with fear."

I knew what that meant. "And all that fear and constriction makes even more density."

"Absolutely. Fear acts as a magnet for density, so the person becomes even more separated from the field of her true being."

"What happens then?"

Quietly, the voice replied, "Personality marches back and forth in its capsule with great energy, trying desperately to get all aspects of life on Earth in order, thinking it will then feel safe."

"And the more energy it diverts, the less it uses to reconnect with the soul?" I knew that one. I had created diversions all my life. Whenever I felt existential anxiety, I started some new project to distract myself. Sometimes it didn't even matter whether my new venture failed or not. Either way, it was a comforting diversion.

There was tremendous love in every word the voice spoke. "You see, safety can never come from outside. The personality knows that. All things on Earth are limited; they come to an end. Depending on something that by definition will not always be there makes for great fear."

"And a lot of middle-of-the-night anxiety attacks," I said.

Softly I heard, "In the night, personality is not as successful at avoiding the awareness that it is a limited, finite being, as are all things of its world."

"Boy, we try hard to avoid thinking about that!" I considered how much energy and time people put into finding the right relationship; the one that would be there for all time. And everyone was frantic about their job security. We were confronted with the evidence of our mortality every day. And we were terrified about death. Our personalities worked frantically to avoid thinking about what appeared to be an indisputable end.

"Why doesn't the soul prevent all of that?" It seemed heartless to allow us to become so lost and unhappy.

"Remember, Earth must always be a place of absolute free will. The moment your soul sends you forth into your time on

Earth, you are free to do what you wish. Your soul will not knock on your capsule and demand that you stop separating yourself. It will wait for you to dissolve the capsule that keeps you apart."

"Even if we make an absolute mess out of our lives?" I didn't want to give up the idea that something was going to rescue me someday from responsibility for my life.

The voice continued to explain. "The energies of the soul are fine and soft, they will not wear away density. The personality has slower energies, the kind that create density. You see, asking your soul to wear down density is like expecting air to break down a stone wall. The air is patient like the soul. It will wait and surround the wall, softly following its every line, curve, and crevice. But it cannot knock the wall down."

"So, you are saying it's up to us to do something about our separation from our souls? Like Daniel told me, calling out to God, or an angel, or some cosmic problem-solver isn't really going to help at all."

"That is correct."

"How do I do it? Tell me, how can I get myself out of that horrible jail cell?" I watched the bubble for movement. It had been a long time since I had seen any sign of life.

The voice answered. "First, your personality, the part you think of as 'me,' must redefine itself. It is only an accessory, an instrument of the soul. You were given a physical body and sent to Earth to work for your soul. Instead of acting like an emperor in its illusionary kingdom, the personality must see itself as an essential part of something tremendously important, vast, and glorious. You see, the role of your personality is to bring back its earthly experiences so that the soul can progress. But the personality is also meant to bring the light of the soul into the relative darkness of your Earth. Your personality can broadcast the pure light of your soul through the density surrounding Earth."

"That sounds beautiful, and so important."

"It is, Karen. Particularly in this time of great distress for Gaia, and increasing confusion of the second-wave beings. Many are searching. The light of your soul, in alignment with your personality, can help others find their way as well."

I was searching for some way out of the mistakes I had made. "So the first step is to practice thinking of myself as an instrument of something much bigger and more important."

Gently, the voice responded, "That is true. You must begin to see yourself as a possession of the soul."

"And see my lifetime as important to the growth of that soul?" That would lend a lot of meaning to my existence! I had always wondered what I was doing here. I think we all wonder. If our awareness didn't include the soul, we spent our time making money and competing for recognition. It was all pretty meaningless when you considered that it all appeared to come to a frightening end.

"And what else will help you reconnect with the greater field of your being?" the voice asked.

"I don't know . . ." I thought for a minute. "Yes, I do know! Getting rid of as much density as I possibly can, making choices in the moment to lessen, rather than increase, my density."

"Very good, Karen."

I went on. "And not feeding my social mind. That's what was splattering density all over the walls of my capsule, wasn't it? All that agitated confusion was my social mind darting here and there, trying to get free. It was only making for itself a stronger prison!"

"Karen, personality generates many illusions. What picture must it present today so that it can win over other human beings? It must win because it must have energy. The energy must come from outside because it has no inner source."

So much made sense now. "The more we cut ourselves off from our soul, the more desperate we are. That's part of the reason for all the terrible violence, isn't it?"

The voice answered. "If you see your personality as your real self, you will only be able to view others just as personalities. When one lost personality, detached in awareness from its soul, encounters another detached personality, there is great potential for physical and psychological violence."

"Because we don't see the whole picture, we don't see that everyone is really an enormous field of energy. We just see some little personality out there trying to take what we need for ourselves. Depending on how frantic we get about what we don't have, we'll do anything to that person to get it."

I had thought about this before in economic terms—the desperate man who can't get a job and commits a crime in order to eat. Then he's begun a pattern he can't break; he becomes increasingly desperate, victimizing others so that he can survive. But this problem was much broader; this involved everybody, not just one segment of society.

The voice responded. "All conflicts between human beings have one place of resolution—in the consciousness of each person, not in the interplay between the two. When detached personalities are busy comparing and competing in their little kingdoms, it truly seems that the only place to resolve interpersonal problems is in the external world. Humans size each other up. Their social minds think about how they can knock their opponent down verbally, even physically.

"But the only place of resolution is within each being. Acknowledge yourself as the spiritual being that you are. Acknowledge the spiritual reality of the other being. Know that his personality is a temporal device, as is yours. Practice seeing that you are both creations of spirit. See the beauty of the soul who sits across from you, even as personality plays grotesque games of power. In this way, conflict with another person can simply be a string around your finger to remind you of your own spiritual work."

Excitement was building inside me. "So we're all trapped in these little spaces, bubbles, capsules, really tombs! We're supposed to be part of an enormous being, not just what our senses can measure."

"Very good."

I didn't want to stay trapped in my tomb. "What else can I do to get free?"

"Begin your practice of setting down density. Begin to practice knowing the truth of what your lifetime is about. This will begin a tiny hole, a way out of your entombment. You have been buried alive, trapped in a lifeless place. You must wish with all your heart to claw your way out and into freedom, for you are alive! You can realize that you exist not only within the boundaries of this body, but outside it as well. You can realize that you exist beyond the boundaries of all the things you have been taught or have seen, touched, tasted, or heard."

I could feel passion rising within me. I wanted to reclaim my existence. "I want to get out!" I cried, emotion charging my words with a force unfamiliar to me.

"That's right, Karen! The cry for freedom must come from within you. No one can give this to you. No one can say, 'Take my passion and use it.' The powerful demand to reclaim who you are must come from inside you!"

Everything was clear in this moment. Like those special days when the light is absolutely perfect and everything in the environment is sharp and full, I could see what was being said. Why hadn't people known this before? Why hadn't we stood up and demanded our birthright?

"What takes us so long to get to this point? We've been robbed by our own social minds! Why have we settled for this kind of existence?" I asked indignantly.

"Like anyone who loses their freedom, you did protest at first. Then you became desperate and frantic. But once people are trapped long enough, they will resign themselves to what seems to be fate, and forget what is true."

I remembered reading somewhere that if you keep flies in a jar with a lid, after a while you can remove the lid and the flies will not go beyond the top of the jar. They have learned they cannot get past a certain point. Once they learn to be trapped, they stay trapped.

"If you practice remembering the truth of your being, and focus an undying passion on breaking free, you will grow bigger than your capsule. You can be a butterfly, with personality as the little bug in the middle and soul the beautiful wings that make it fly. And if you keep going, you will find yourself with beautiful colored wings on either side, lifting you as high as you wish to go and as far as you wish to fly . . ."

My heart was already flying. I could be free again! I didn't have to be trapped in the human condition. None of us had to stay in our personal prisons. I didn't know how I was going to do it yet, but I could learn. I was ready to do whatever it took. No one could afford to be passive any longer. We all had to break for freedom! It was time to stand up and reclaim our truth. We had only our illusions to lose and limitless love and energy to gain.

I bent down, and scooped up a huge handful of glorious golden light, and sent it straight up into the air. I yelled with all the power I could find in my being. "I want it! I want it back! It's mine and I want it back!"

With that, the ugly mottled bubble cracked and fell open. The woman unfurled herself and, filled with an awesome she stepped out into the magnificent field of light.

❧ TWENTY-EIGHT ❧

"Hi!"

Turning around quickly, I was astounded to see Daniel walking toward me, gold and silver light bouncing from his bare feet. "You're out of the bubble! That's so good, Karen!"

"It's wonderful!" I exclaimed. "I don't quite understand how I did it, but it is wonderful."

On the news, I had seen rehabilitated eagles being released back into the wild. I had silently cried as I saw a crated symbol of freedom carried off a truck and up a forest trail. I imagined its fear at being hopelessly caught in the hands of strangers, their kind having been responsible for its injuries. But at last the moment would come. The door would sweep open, and the bird would peer outside. It scarcely believed it could go home again. Then, with a magnificent wild cry and a burst of its wings, away it would fly. Joy would rain down from the sky as the bird left its sorrow and rushed heavenward. I knew now why my tears had come.

Daniel looked at me solemnly and said, "Let's see if you can stay out."

I could hardly believe my ears. "What do you mean? Once I'm out, I'm out. Right?" I felt a deep sadness in the pit of my stomach that I realized had been there for a very long time. Now that I was free, I didn't ever want to end up like that again.

"Nope." He had a way of saying the most difficult things with a single word.

"You mean I could get trapped all over again?" I already knew the answer.

He spoke one enormously frightening word. "Yep."

I felt like a prisoner who had broken free only to find his captors waiting in the dark, having known his plan all along. "Please, Daniel, come on, help me out a little. How could that happen?"

"Remember how tricky your social mind was?" He kicked up a few effervescent beams with his foot. Spectacular blue, violet, and orange particles of light flew high into the air and floated back to the ground. I couldn't help noticing the terrible disparity between this beauty and the ugliness of my capsule.

"Yes, of course I do, " I responded with a vehemence that surprised even me. "It's responsible for so much human misery. I know that now."

"It can sneak right up on you again. And before you know it"—he clapped his hands—"you're trapped."

"It sounds like I have to keep watching out all the time." All right, if that's what I needed to do, so be it. I wasn't going back, not now.

"Really, you just have to remember all the time that it's there. Don't let it get away with anything. The minute something comes into your head that is hurtful to you or someone else, a judgment or a comparison, throw it right out! If you let the social mind get its hands on something negative, it will multiply. And I don't think you can afford to let even one splatter of density begin to spread."

"God, I could see how awful it was. When I was in the bubble, that dark stuff just keep getting thicker and thicker, until I couldn't even see myself in there anymore. And I'm sure I couldn't see out."

I remembered the tragic desperation I had witnessed. It was far worse than anything I had seen before. No wonder we suffer emotionally and physically. No wonder most of us don't dare to say how unhappy we are inside.

Daniel nodded sadly. "You miss even seeing your own soul, let alone being with it, like you are right now."

"This is so incredibly wonderful, Daniel. I want to have it for the rest of my life." Despite my sadness and fear at even a mention of the idea that I could find myself back in the capsule, I had never felt so full of joy as I did right now. In the midst of my own vast soul, there was profound beauty, love, safety, and security. I was being given something no human being could ever provide. Nothing I could gain from another person, nothing I could feel from any accomplishment, nothing I could ever produce could even approximate this happiness. That's what I wanted now. Anything else, no matter how grand the social mind might think it was, would be only an empty reminder of how far away I had sent my soul.

The little boy looked at me a moment. "You don't really have to make your social mind an enemy. It's more that you must honor your true self. You wouldn't let your body get all mucked up day after day and not wash it."

"Of course not," I replied, making a face at the thought of being so dirty.

"Same thing."

Okay, so I didn't have to live in a state of war with my social mind. I, after all, had the real power if I would just use it consistently. I had seen it in my experience with that miserable, mean woman inside me. Once I had stood up and told her to stop, she had obeyed. But I also remembered that she had attacked Adam for energy the first chance she got.

Then a wonderful thought occurred to me. "You said something about bringing that light into life on Earth . . . for other people?"

"Yep. When you are clear and clean, your soul's energy begins to shine right through you, just like the way you were on the beach. Weren't you beautiful? Don't you think it would be fantastic for some of this light to be in the world?" He bent over and sent handfuls of tiny emerald and gold incandescent spheres raining down over us. The light was glorious. My skin was again transparent, my heart turning and light flowing from me in every direction. I remembered how it had lit up the darkness. "It could help other people and Gaia, too."

A smile crossed Daniel's face. "See, keepers of the buildings, you know, the religious leaders, mostly only make big speeches about the concept of spirit. Nothing really changes. Nobody gets any closer to their soul. You know what? It's just as easy for social minds to use spirituality as a subject to make themselves stronger as it is for them to use something else."

I considered a peculiar thought I had never shared with anyone. Taking a breath, I said, "Well, now that you mention it, spiritual people have always been kind of a pain in the neck. I hate to say that, but . . . do you know what I mean?" What was it? Spiritual people always seemed smug and superior, like the cat who swallowed the canary. It was maddening. In response, I had acted like I had the same level of spiritual awareness that they appeared to have. But I really didn't.

The people who were coming across that way didn't have it either. It was just their social minds with another script, another strategy to grab energy. While I was busy feeling spiritually inadequate, their social minds were stealing energy from Adam like crazy. That why I felt such dread when the topic came up! It had all been a sham. Just another of the social mind's exercises to reveal who was strongest.

Daniel broke into my thoughts. "Karen, you're doing so well!"

I was excited, feeling I might actually be on my way to permanent liberation. "Daniel, are you saying that if the social mind is out of the way, we would be able to consistently offer each other the kind of love that exists right here in the soul?"

"Of course you could; that's the whole point!" He grinned at me enthusiastically.

"And, correct me if I'm wrong, but we wouldn't have to necessarily say a single word about anything spiritual at all, would we?" My heart was beginning to pound. A new vision of the world was beginning to take shape in my mind.

"Nope." He continued to smile.

Now I was smiling, too. "That's a revolutionary idea! All of this has absolutely nothing to do with pious words, or threats of punishment, or praying hard enough or believing scripture, or any of that! And it doesn't have to do with calling on angels to come and save us. It's all personal work, isn't it? All this time it has been about battling the social mind and breaking free into the surrounding field of our own soul!"

"Yep," he said.

"Daniel, that could change everything!" I said, barely able to contain myself.

After all, what could happen if all the churches turned into centers for learning about how to get rid of the social mind, instead of posturing halls for that social mind? Suppose ministers learned how to access their own soul energies, instead of pretending they understood a whole bunch of esoteric material that was cruel, even bloody in nature? And what if we could gather together and simply fill ourselves and each other with tangible energies of love like the men on the beach had offered me?

If that vengeful Earth god was removed from our shoulders

and we took back our own power, nothing would ever be the same again!

"Daniel you're talking about a whole new chance for mankind! If the social mind is removed from power, and we all learn to be what we were meant to be, everything would change! All our garbled directions for living could be replaced with energies of the soul. Can you imagine what kinds of communities we could create together? That old dream of caring for each other, making sure no one goes hungry, knowing how much we are all loved and never forgotten. My God, that's possible, isn't it?"

"That's what we've tried so hard to tell you all along." He continued with renewed seriousness. "But I have to tell you, the social mind is a terrible opponent. It kills the teachers and hides the truth. It demands that things be proven in the realm of density."

"You're talking about how we don't trust anyone who tries to help us sort all this out. We always want to see a miracle—a mountain moving, instant cures to disease, things like that?"

I had felt that way myself. But other social minds were out there, waiting to capitalize on that need. So many ministries were all about desperate people looking for proof that God exists. I thought about a recent news report that said a thousand people had tried to barge into someone's backyard. They had heard that a voice was coming out of the hot tub there. It wasn't that the voice was saying anything helpful or profound, it was just the "miracle" that had people going.

"See, showing off won't get anyone anywhere. All it can accomplish is to make people worship somebody. That's the opposite direction from where you need to look. Going outside to make a parade behind another person will never, ever take you home."

"But Jesus did some of that." I thought silently, please don't start challenging what Jesus did. That's the one thing that hasn't been touched today.

"Actually, he didn't," Daniel said quietly.

"What?" I started to shake.

"Just a good marketing campaign," the little boy replied. As I stared after him in astonishment, he walked away, his small body disappearing into the diffused silver light.

❧ TWENTY-NINE ❧

"Wait! Please, wait!" I ran after him in desperation, rapidly finding myself lost in an ultraviolet fog. There it was, that sensation of my mind falling to one side. I would not be surprised if it finally found its way through my ear and onto the ground. In fact, it was quite amazing I had any brain left at this point.

"Daniel, where are you? For God's sake, don't leave me with that!" I looked frantically around me, unable to see anything. Then it occurred to me. "Okay. I'm in the middle of my own soul. I don't have to panic. I don't have to build a capsule just because I'm afraid." I took in a deep breath and felt an immediate calming sensation flow like warm honey through my body. "I'm perfectly all right. If I stayed here forever, I would be absolutely all right."

"Good, Karen!" Daniel seemed to take form immediately in front of me. Holding an ice cream cone, he licked some of the dark, rich chocolate from his thumb.

"How do you do that?" I was momentarily distracted by his ability to simply materialize. He had an ice cream cone. We were standing in the middle of my soul and he had an ice cream cone! I steadied my mind and aimed it toward more important things. "Wait. I want to know what you meant back there when you said Jesus didn't do the miracles and it was just a marketing thing."

Taking an enormous bite, he casually said, "Just confused

stories that people started using so they could have more power. My goodness, your Bible is an awful mess."

I spoke very slowly to buy myself some time, "What are you saying?"

"Well, have you ever actually read the New Testament?"

"Sure," I answered quickly. "Of course I have." Seeing that he knew I wasn't completely telling the truth, I added, "I can't say I could tell you exactly what's in it."

"See! That's part of the problem. You think you know what's there, but you don't even read it. If you did, maybe some lights would go on! They have Jesus saying really terrible stuff about punishment and eternal damnation and how you have to follow a God who acts like he hates all of you . . . things like that."

"That does sound familiar."

"You guys leave everything up to the religious leaders and never really look at it for yourselves. If you took the time to examine that document, you'd see how really cruel it sounds. How could that be right?"

Instinctively, I felt that I should defend the most hallowed work of our civilization. "But isn't there a lot about how we can be saved from all of that if we follow Jesus? Isn't that what he came to do, save us all from death, and from the punishment we deserve?" Wait a minute, we had already talked about this. Why would a loving God send his son to die so that he wouldn't kill us all?

"Nope," he said, taking the last bite of the sugar cone.

"Why did he come, then?"

Drawing a forearm across his mouth to wipe the chocolate away, he answered, "To teach everybody the same things I've been trying to tell you about."

I felt light-headed. "Daniel, are you telling me that the words of Jesus, even the miracles ascribed to Jesus, aren't true?"

"Yep."

That thunderbolt was out there somewhere. I knew it in my bones. My voice trembled. "Maybe you'd better tell me what he did say and do."

"He came to teach you about density, and the capsule, and your social mind and the soul that surrounds you. Like I said, just what I've been trying to tell you about. It's not that he didn't help people heal their bodies; of course he did, but not through miracles." Surveying the dazed expression on my face, he said, "Maybe I better tell you about how it all got so mixed up."

"That would be good," I said shakily.

"Two things—density and power."

"Okay." That seemed like the least dangerous response I could generate.

"See, lots of people didn't understand what Jesus was saying in the first place. That's what happens when we try to teach you guys. If you're locked into density, and rely only on your senses, then that's how you experience and understand everything." He shrugged his small shoulders and looked at me as if I would have something intelligent to add.

"Okay." Again, safety seemed the best option, and I looked at him with the same expectation.

He continued his explanation. "So Jesus talked, and some people were able to understand it and some weren't."

"Because some were more trapped in density than others?" Good. I was actually all right, so far. I understood what he was saying, and it wasn't that bad.

He took it a step further. "Yep. All that stuff about coming to die for your sins so you could be forever saved in the kingdom of heaven . . . well, that's not what he said at all."

"What did he say?" I decided to go for it. After all, I had

to know as much as I could if I was going to stay out of that capsule.

"It was all about density. If you don't choose to set it down, then you have to live alone in your capsule and you never experience the joy and love that surrounds you. That's what he meant by the kingdom of heaven. It's right here! It's with you all the time. You're the one who locks yourself up in a dark little room. Your soul doesn't move away from you. And if you live all separated like that, you're going to be awfully scared about death. That's why the story about the resurrection got started."

"The story . . ." Courage leaked out the soles of my feet.

He nodded. "Jesus did come in a body, just like all human beings. And the people with lots of horrible density killed that body. But the body didn't come back. Why would that be necessary? Who wants to stay in their little container?"

The lessons of my childhood church would not give way easily. "The resurrection . . . he rose on the third day . . . that's not true?"

"Well, kind of, sort of, not exactly . . ." He gazed off for a moment. "See, all along he kept trying to tell people all about who they really were, just like I've been trying to tell you. Finally, Jesus said:

" 'Okay, all right, tell you what . . . people around here are getting pretty upset with what I've been saying. So, I'm going to let it come to its inevitable dense end. I bet they'll kill me. And then I'll show you that what I've been saying all along is true. People, you are not your body! You do not end when it does! Furthermore, you can connect with your own timeless, immortal self while you are still in your body if you stop being so addicted to your social mind and get on with the work you have to do!'

"That's what he said. And guess what happened?"

"Some of them got it and a lot didn't."

"And know what else?"

"No."

"That worked well for people with active social minds who were waiting to grab some of the fame and power that they thought Jesus had."

"What do you mean?"

"Well," he said, sounding a little exasperated, "people are so scared about death, they figured they could just make the resurrection thing literal. Everybody would be impressed if Jesus' actual physical body showed up again, not just his spirit. They figured if they were the ones who actually saw the live, dead body walking around and the other people didn't, well . . ."

Forcefully, I responded, "They would be important. People would feel their only connection with that miracle was through the ones who were right there to see it."

"Bingo. And the next thing you know, those who claimed to have seen the actual body said they were the only ones whom people should follow around. Once these few died, the people who had followed them around said that they should have all the power, and that everybody should only follow them around and there you go . . . the Catholic church."

"What?" I was not a Catholic, but I knew enough about it to be sure you shouldn't take it lightly. After all, it had been around for two thousand years.

"Yep. Invincible popes, bishops, priests, and deacons. People were told that they had the truth, because they all knew somebody who knew somebody who knew somebody who actually saw the body walking around after it was dead. 'Catholic' simply means universal. In other words, they're in charge, there can be only one way of looking at things. And furthermore, if you don't follow them, they won't tell you what that truth is, and then . . ."

"God will punish you and you'll end up in hell." The deception of the ages was beginning to dawn on me. "But the body itself did not rise from the dead?"

"No. But who cares?" he said, shocking me with his ability to overturn cherished beliefs with a single phrase. "Isn't it a whole lot more important to understand that you are more than your body right this very second? Not when it dies, not later when you get saved by somebody, but right now!"

My battered mind took a last stab at protecting itself. "You're reinterpreting the Bible, for God's sake!"

"Well, no, actually I'm explaining an important part of the Bible for man's sake." He looked at me innocently. "Jesus was one of the greatest teachers human beings have ever had. Don't you think it's important for people to understand what he actually said? Why should the people of Earth be left to try to live the distortions of his teaching contained in the Bible? It's so mixed up, all it creates is pain and lost time. That's what he came to save you from: being lost!"

"Save us from being lost?" I gulped hard and said, "It doesn't have the same punch as the story of him being crucified to save us from death and punishment at the hand of an angry God!"

Daniel threw his hands high in the air and yelled, "That's what I mean; that's how it happened! You know what else? It's not even consistent. Do you know who was the very first person to see Jesus after his physical body was destroyed?"

"No. I guess I should have paid more attention in Sunday school."

His eyes shining with excitement at being able to set things straight again, he explained, "Well, it was someone who had listened carefully while Jesus was trying to teach people. It was

someone who didn't lie about seeing him walk around in a physical body after it was crucified. It was someone who had learned
how to see beyond physical reality, and so was able to see Jesus
even after his body was gone."

"Who, Daniel? Tell me, who was it?"

He smiled. "It was a woman. Do you think they included
her when they said people should only follow those who actually saw him?"

"Probably not." After all, even in today's world, we had a
hard time giving women credit for anything.

He shrugged his shoulders and continued. "No, they didn't.
They lied. They claimed to have seen an actual, physical resurrection from the dead. They didn't see that because it didn't
happen! They dismissed her perceptions as imaginary, just like
you guys ignore what you can't see with your eyes."

"Are you saying the physical resurrection story was a lie,
something made up by a bunch of people who only wanted
power?"

"Yep."

"But there was someone who saw Jesus, not in his 'risen
from the dead' physical body, but beyond that body? Somebody
who had learned from him about how to see beyond what can
be seen with the eyes?"

"Yep. Yet to this day, the Catholic church tells people to
follow a succession of authority that is based on those who
actually saw the physical body moving around after it was crucified—but doesn't allow women into the priesthood, even
though a woman was the first one to honestly and truly see him.
Know why?"

I gave it a try. "Prevailing sexist attitudes?"

"In a way," he said. "But it's worse than that."

My stomach reacted with a familiar alert. "What do you
mean?"

He charged ahead. "Well, that's where the masculine way of seeing things took over most of the world."

"What?" I felt as if I had started down the steep side of a roller coaster.

Showing no mercy, he went on. "God was established in your Old Testament as masculine. But Jesus shook all of that up right away. He made it perfectly clear that it didn't matter at all whether your soul created a female or a male body. The men who wanted the power didn't want that out there at all. The last thing they could afford was to have the Son of God running around telling everybody women were equal."

Receiving only a dazed expression as a response, he continued, "Anyway, a woman was one of the people who understood what Jesus was really talking about. Want to know why?"

"Of course I want to know why . . ." I answered weakly.

"Because she used feminine ways of knowing things to hear what Jesus meant when he taught—you know, intuition, emotion, listening to her inner voice and inductive reasoning."

"So, Jesus' teachings were more in line with feminine abilities? But, Daniel, what about all of the men? Didn't he come to help them, too?"

"Oh, Karen, all of this division between male and female is so silly. Really, all of you are both. You all have complete ways of knowing and understanding things, but then you look at your body and decide what to throw out depending on what parts you have. That's pretty dumb, don't you think?"

I nodded in agreement and waited for him to continue.

"Well, the rightful leader of the church, if there was going to be a church, wasn't Peter at all. He was only one of the people who misunderstood what Jesus said. He took everything very literally, and by doing that, he missed the whole point."

The sensibility I had left began to wave a white flag. "Are you saying what I think you are saying?"

He went straight for the knees. "The rightful leader was Mary Magdalene."

My defenses crumpled. "Daniel, my God, the former prostitute?"

"Lover of Jesus . . . body, mind, and spirit," he said simply.

I managed a squeak. "Oh, God."

"Well, of course he had a lover. He had the body of a grown man. Why wouldn't he want to be loved in that way?" This point seemed perfectly obvious to Daniel, but it was directly contrary to everything we had been taught.

"I need to sit down," I said, finding myself already cross-legged on the field of light. It was so lovely here, sparkling drifts of pink and violet light made their way over me like dandelion dust on a summer's day. I had to bring my mind back to hear Daniel continuing the story.

"So anyway, *she* should have been the leader—not because she was so close to him, but because she truly understood what he was saying. But they wouldn't let her. Most of them only heard with the masculine mind. They took everything Jesus said absolutely literally. All that beautiful poetry, his wonderful way of explaining things to people who were so lost . . . it all was understood to be literal.

"Not only that," he added. "By not wanting to hear Jesus when he talked about the equality between men and women, they reinforced the masculine concept of God. God remained a big, awful father in the sky, patriarchal, punishing, law dispensing. Justice, vengeance, power over other people . . . male stuff, the kind of stuff that has to be reckoned with by the same kinds of energies. So the only right way to deal with things became through the rational, sensory mind. And the value of feminine elements went right out the window."

"Let me see if I understand this. You're saying we made the masculine viewpoint a God and proceeded to worship both the figure we created and that way of looking at reality. But what we needed was to include both masculine and feminine abilities?"

"Exactly. The masculine energy provided the organizational abilities that it took to get the Christian message all over the world. It provided the focused drive that it took to make sure that they kept going until everyone heard what they had to say. The masculine energy did the recording, the ordering of information, the making sure that people got all the information. The only problem was, it was incorrect information. They hadn't heard it right in the first place!"

I shook my head as if it could help me somehow. "I need to make sure you're not talking about men and women here."

"No. I'm not saying it was men's fault. I'm saying you guys decided that only a certain kind of energy was acceptable. Then you threw out the part that would have allowed you to understand Jesus. And since you didn't understand what he said, the confused message was solidified into a masculine energy church with male people in charge of it."

I could hardly believe we hadn't seen these things for ourselves. "And then we used those directions in the mixed-up Bible, as you told me before, to form our communities, our nations, our relationships with each other."

Grief filled his eyes. "And you used that unbalanced masculine energy to run all over the Earth demanding that people believe the same thing as you do and killing those who didn't."

The Crusades, the Inquisition, the destruction of native cultures around the globe—much of it had been in the name of the church. And we were attacking our very home. "Wait a minute! If we exclude the feminine, we're excluding Gaia!"

"Yep. That's why you treat her the way you do, with the same disrespect you have for all that's feminine. You run over her, try to control her, abuse her, don't listen to her, take from her without concern about how she's going to be afterward."

"That sounds like feminist politics," I said warily.

"Actually, I'm sorry to say this, but feminist politics is really just more worship of masculine energies."

"What?"

"Yep," he said. "Feminism is just saying that masculine energies should be used by people in female bodies as much as by people in male bodies. Feminists don't like feminine energy any better than anyone else."

While I was mulling that over, something else occurred to me. "Daniel, does this have something to do with why we are so homophobic? Gay people are tremendously persecuted."

"Yep. People dislike the female energy they see in gay men, and dislike the male energy they see coming from lesbians. People only feel safe if male energy is confined to male people and female energy is confined to female people. That way, it's easier to identify and keep the female energy under control. But like I said, you all really have both kinds of energies."

I took a deep breath. "Tell me some more of what Jesus really had to say about humanity's predicament."

"Okay," he answered agreeably. "Well let's see, first of all, your Bible and your keepers insist on telling people that God is way, way out there somewhere. And you guys are all these little, pitiful things that are going to be squashed one day if you don't shape up."

"Jesus didn't agree?"

He grinned at me and said, "Of course not, silly! You're divine energy. The energy of the all flows continuously through your soul. The only thing that makes you pitiful and small is your own social mind and your dedication to the worship of it and creating a capsule and then mucking it all up with density."

My courage was rising. "And this issue of needing to be saved?"

"Well, you do need that, but not in the way people have been led to believe. You need to be saved from your misunderstanding and your desperate attempts to protect yourselves by building walls of density. And we keep trying to save you by giving you all the information you need, by giving you visionary experiences, providing you encouragement, and sending our love. But *you* have to decide to break out of your own capsule and your own social mind. You created it; it's yours to maintain or destroy."

"So, what about the idea that we're sinful and Jesus wants us to repent and accept salvation?"

He shrugged his shoulders. "Well, it's all garbled up. Remember, sin means to be apart from God, or apart from your soul. So, the mechanisms that allow for that are density and the social mind. You punish yourselves by remaining apart from everything that can sustain you."

I was on a roll now. "Salvation?"

"That means to rejoin . . ." He stopped. His face was full of love. "Rejoin your soul, be as a little child in the arms of one who loves you so deeply and so completely that you could never want for anything again."

That heavy word "salvation," the idea that had tormented us for hundreds of years—all it meant was to come home! I had to ask, "Jesus actually talked about that? About rejoining?"

"Well, sure! His words were all about learning that the social mind exists—the way out requires opening up your heart, not constricting with fear."

I took a deep breath. "Are you saying that Jesus was a guide, a teacher who simply wanted to tell us how we could melt our capsule and have a reunion with the soul?"

"Yep," he replied, watching shock waves pass through me

again. "Know what? One thing Jesus kept telling them over and over again was 'I am not your master.' Boy, did that ever get mixed up!"

"Wait a minute; church people are always saying you have to make Jesus your Lord and Master!"

"I know," he said sadly. "That's pretty terrible because it makes you look outside, and inside is where it all is. See, Jesus told them that! He said, 'I can show you guys how to do it, I'll tell you, I'll even light the way with my own soul energies through this body, but you have to do it yourselves. Don't follow me around and hope I'll take care of it for you. I can't. Wouldn't be right at all.' "

"Why did they record it in the opposite way? The way I've heard it, Jesus tells them they have to follow him or it's all over, over now and over in eternity!"

"I know, Karen. Think how frustrating it is for us to see it all end up like that! If someone is your master, you don't have to think for yourself. You simply do what he tells you. And if that master is gone, you do what his successors tell you to do. And then they have you. You're cut off from your own freedom, your own abilities, your own capacity to be what you were meant to be."

"Daniel," I said, climbing to my feet, "are you saying our whole religious tradition is just the politics of power?"

"Not all of it, but most of it. That's what happens when people just try to find a leader and follow him around. Reconnection with the soul is something you have to do. We can help. We have always tried to help, but you have to do it."

"Jesus didn't want people to rely on him?"

"He tried to prevent all of that, all the worshipping and following, but even that was misunderstood. It's recorded as his being unwilling to stand up and say clearly who he was. He wanted you all to learn how to have access to your own souls."

He waited for my knees to quit shaking and then continued. "See, the purpose of a spiritual teacher is to help you learn to rejoin with your own soul. You're supposed to outgrow him. Then he should say good-bye. Jesus wasn't your master. If you had to keep being dependent on him telling you what to do, that would really mean he was an awful teacher."

"But that is so contrary to what we've been told!"

He nodded. "Once you know your own soul, you're the same as Jesus. You know who you really are just like he did. See, the resurrection story wasn't somebody's weird fantasy. It's an important story, but it's really about getting out of the dead world of your capsule. If you're captured in walls of density, with no connection to love and beauty—that's like being dead. I guess you could say that life the way most of you live it is death, and death is life."

I shivered, remembering the sight of myself desperately trying to get out of that prison. "Living in the capsule, you're cut off, covered with density, suffocating."

"Yep. By showing himself after his body was destroyed, Jesus was just demonstrating the reality of what truly exists, who you really are, and how to get there so you can be free and alive again."

I found a little smile. "So it's really more similar to the teachings of the east, about the illusions of the world and the need for enlightenment."

To my surprise, he wrinkled his face in distaste. "Actually, people mixed those teachings up too, in an awful way."

"Those are garbled, too?" When I thought about it, this made sense. People following the Koran, or the Talmud, or other religious teachings weren't doing any better than we were. They had the same problems of violence, poverty, anxiety, alienation.

The little boy interrupted my thoughts. "But who do you

think the masters of the east were?" He watched me, blue eyes sparkling with anticipation.

"I have no idea."

"Of course you do, Karen!" He began to laugh and twirled around, arms outstretched, lifting his head upward, as if to the sun. "It's all us! It's always been us!"

Suddenly the light field began to shift and change, like an ocean enlivened by a storm. Great waves of light swept back and forth, beautiful beyond human experience. The enormous sea began to find form in ultraviolet blue, pink, yellow, silver, and gold.

As if heaven itself had opened, a great light appeared. Golden rays streamed toward me, and I shielded my eyes by instinct. But I didn't need to, for this was the light of purest love. Still, I was afraid until I saw in that light a luminous presence—now almost clear, now almost gone. It was a child, a glorious child. Light poured from her heart, radiated from her eyes. And in her hands, she held the Earth.

I watched, awestruck, as she became a man. His hands held all the stars, and with immense joy he scattered them outward and they became planets, spinning in the darkness. Then he became a boy-child holding a wooden cross, bloody and worn. And I knew for the first time what it symbolized. The horizontal arms were our life on the Earth, the vertical beam represented our journey out of density home again to our soul. The child smiled and drew a circle around the middle with a spectacular blue light. I knew at last that circle was my heart, the meeting place of the heavens and the Earth.

The child walked toward me, shifting form a thousand times as he approached, now the Jesus of my childhood, now the Buddha I had learned of as I grew, and now all the other teachers of Earth. In magnificent harmony, male, female, black, white, red, brown, and yellow, they moved in and out of one another.

They were all one teacher. There had never been any change in the message we were given. There was no confusion, except that which we had brought with us when we tried to hear. The message did not need to be different because it was ultimately so simple.

"Please come home. Do not live alone and in pain. You are loved beyond all you can imagine. We long for each of you, waiting for you as the son and daughter lost long ago. We surround you forever, wishing with a mighty heart that you may open the door of the prison you have made, and at last . . . at last, come home."

I fell to my knees and sobbed, reaching out my arms to this woman-man-child who loved me so much. The luminous presence became a sphere, spinning toward me, shimmering, whirling red and silver light. It entered my heart and exploded ecstatically. I heard without sound, "Never be afraid, I am with you always . . ."

❦ THIRTY ❧

"The infinite heart turns, quiet and full. You are contained forever in that heart. Turn your own heart as we have shown you. Turn in harmony with the infinite one. Come, all hearts from across your world, turn in love with Gaia, the being from heaven whose love is strong enough to help you find your way home.

"Gaia waits, as all the beings of heaven wait, for you to choose. Each of your actions is noticed, and there is great celebration for each choice you make that leads you home. Never think you are not longed for. Never think the arms do not wait. Never think the infinite heart does not know where you are."

My hands had been taken by the boy-child, and he led me into the great light; I held no fear of going. The boundaries of my being melted into his. It no longer mattered who I had been; I was going home. Forever they had waited for me with a patience beyond that of all mankind put together. And now it was time for me to return home.

I went, my body shattering into a million particles of light, only a heart left, only a heart held by two small hands. And the cross had dissolved, leaving behind only the blue circle that now surrounded me. Activated by pure joy, the light that was me danced in celebration with all that surrounded me. The endlessly moving, mighty heart beat now and forever, its deep rhythm caressing my being with incredible love. And, Karen the capsule woman was no more, and it did not matter. I was going home.

The boy-child now smiled as wide as the universe. My heart gazed from its position in his hands upward into his face, and knew at last why he had come.

"We get another chance, don't we?" With no voice, my heart had dared to ask the unthinkable. The boy-child's love cascaded over me and, ecstatically, I received confirmation that there was more than enough love to offer mankind another chance.

"What can I do? What do you wish from me?"

My heart looked to find the Earth in the same hands. I could hear Earth's people calling desperately for the help of the angry god, and I saw that their pain and panic could lead them nowhere, even as mine had never done.

"What do you wish from me?"

Traveling into the spellbinding light, I could see Earth's people, caught in their capsules, struggling in agony and fear. But, here and there, I could see a heart wheel turning—clogged and filled with debris, but turning. And where there was such a heart, soul light came into the world. And where there was soul light, Gaia's creatures were healthy and green. The people around such a heart were awakened and beginning to stumble on their own journey to freedom.

"What can I do?"

Suddenly I knew I was going into the realm of heaven. I did not know if I would ever create my body again, but I did not care. Through the beams of silver, gold, pink, and violet light we traveled, with my heart, the center of all that I was, still held in the hands of the boy child. I looked out across the light to the edge where I could see darkness. And in that darkness, beautiful, shimmering, translucent, souls were separated, now looking for the unity of long ago, the home from which they had become lost.

"What do you wish from me?"

My heart swelled and wept for the tragedy of it all. There had been such misunderstanding, fear, anguish, and suffering on the Earth. And I knew at once that the only way home was through the heart of Gaia. That was why she had come. My heart's tears transformed into shooting beams of silver light, and I watched them skip over the hands of the boy-child and out into forever.

"What can I do?"

Earth's people had to find the strength and desire that could power a tremendous cry for freedom as deep and as mighty as anything we had ever known. We must throw off the mantle of ignorance and refuse to remain separated from the truth of our being.

I knew we must look within and never stop until we had gone so far within that we were past the capsule. It was not enough to be self-consumed with concerns of the capsule, as our physicians and counselors had taught us to be. "Within" did not mean apart from the world, selfish and self-absorbed; it meant true destruction of what we had thought of as self. The social mind had to be starved into extinction. We could not continue to feed it, but had to find ways to send it away forever.

We went forward together, the luminous path opening wide. Abundant, beckoning energy filled my heart until I was standing again on my own. Still, all that remained of me was my heart, now able to direct itself to service sustained by indescribable love.

I was ready to receive my instruction, knowing the ultimate stage of my growth could only be service to humanity. I could only do this in freedom from my capsule. I could only do this by bringing my soul's energies straight into the Earthtime.

We went farther into the calling and the longing and the love, and it strengthened and sustained me. I had no need to look back to the past, to what I had been. It had blown away, as inconsequential as dust on a towering tree.

Pure love awaited me and awakened me even more, and I remembered! At once, I remembered!

The infinite heart is filled with the love that animates all things. From that mighty place of love is sent forth the breath that makes life in all things. And so, love is the first force and life is the second. As you exist on your Earth, know that each breath is propelled by love. And while you are on Earth, notice that between each breath there is a small silence. Know that in that silence is infinite love that goes nowhere and is never empty. You may draw forth that love with your inhalation and send that breath of life back as a gift to the mighty heart as you exhale. In this way, there is a sacred circle, repeated hundreds of times in each of your days upon the Earth.

You see, your lifetimes are only circles, drawing forth a vehicle to use in your journey to transformation and returning that vehicle when you are through. It is always, and will forever be, but only a drawing forth from the silence of love that animates all things and a giving back, even as your breath is pulled in, used, and given back.

Ahead of me lay pure glory unbound and unfettered. Only sparkling freedom and an endless wellspring of love waited for me to arrive. My own soul welcomed me and took my heart's hands in his and hers and whispered, "Welcome, my sweet child, my creation, my beautiful daughter-son, welcome home, welcome back to the heart of all hearts. You have done well. Thank you for your service to my evolution. Thank you for your willingness to hear me, to move in ways that I asked. I bless your existence in the Earthtime.

"Your life has not rushed inexorably toward death, but your

soul has ever moved toward you. Without interruption, I have whispered to you. In the silence of night, in the emptiness of life's pain, I have quietly sustained you.

"I am yours, a lover whose destination is the center of your heart. Once thought forever gone, the union is again before you. Watch as glorious waves of joy and love encompass you as all souls sing, and everywhere hearts lift as one lost finds home again.

"What is real can never be truly lost, and all that is not real can do nothing in its presence but fall away. See my eyes filled with boundless compassion, unsurpassable love, glorious purpose, coming to meet only with yours. There is no reason to fear, for you see, nothing, no thing is unforgivable in the eyes of the soul.

"Come now . . . come straight into the embrace that has waited for you alone. Come into this sacred place and know me. Infuse your life with the light of its rightful owner. And as light fuses once again with light, only then will you find peace forever."

My heart exploded into infinite showers of love and transformed again; I knew I would see more.

We arrived in the place where all lifetimes are born. A gentle wind wafted across a great plain, and I saw millions of sparkling souls gathered together in loving groups. Thousands of light-filled beings were hard at work. Like magical weavers, they pulled infinitesimal strands of gossamer energy out of themselves, and spun them into wondrously beautiful patterns. Each creation was beautifully unique.

"These are the souls of humanity," my heart whispered.

"Why, of course they are," a soft voice answered. "You see, they are preparing to send forth lifetimes to the Earth."

As I watched, the souls released gold and silver light and created Adams and the second spirit that would allow each person to have his or her "I am alive" consciousness. They poured love through each strand and softly sighed the breath of life into each one.

We stopped before a dazzling soul, and my heart swelled with joy as she pulled a thousand glimmering silver threads from her heart and gently whirled them into spirals. As she worked, more glorious light sped down the fibers, filling them with astonishing beauty.

With incredible passion, this glorious being created her coming lifetime. I watched in wonder as she produced minuscule beads of sparkling amber, turquoise, and deep purple. She attached those tiny spheres to the spiraled strands. Slowly, each one began to rotate around the strands like the Moon around the Earth.

"What are those?" my heart asked, overwhelmed by the profound care the soul poured into her creation.

Looking over at me with luminous eyes, she whispered a love-filled secret. "You see, each person has at his or her core all the instructions for a lifetime on Earth."

"Everything is predestined?" my heart murmured.

"No, everything exists as potential," she responded. "It is up to the human being to amplify those instructions into a life of beauty or deny them. But you see, no matter what you do, no matter who you are, you are forever pure love. That is how we have made you, and that is what you truly are."

The enormous plain seemed to extend into forever. Layers of radiant light illuminated this place with the transparent colors of the rainbow. Glorious souls were clustered together in loving groups, and suddenly, I understood that each soul belonged to a community of purpose. Each community existed to further the soul's evolution.

In the midst of the gracious love of each community, souls carefully created their intricate patterns. Glorious, incandescent matrixes were born of each soul's specific purpose. Like dew caught on a spider's web, glowing particles of light clung to each pattern. Dancing inside each particle was an intimate knowledge of the soul's community, carefully woven into the very fiber of the coming human being. In this way, it would be possible for him or her to find meaning and purpose during his or her lifetime.

I drifted on the shimmering wind, deeply comforted by the knowledge that each person comes to Earth with everything he needs for his successful journey. Only by acting in accordance with the intent of his soul could he find true fulfillment and joy in existence on Earth.

I heard the newborn cries of a thousand beings, and saw in their eyes the reflection of the soul. I heard their hearts call out, "Do not leave me here! Do not leave me in this little space! I want only to be with you, forever and ever." And the spirits calmed those hearts, silencing their cries with gentle words. "Do not be afraid, I am with you always."

My heart went farther and I heard unique music, traveling for all time, carrying the melodious message of each soul community.

"First Step" sang to me. The souls of this community spent their times on Earth helping others to find the first steps on the path homeward. They lived in service to humanity's awakening. They softly blew on the small fires in the hearts of men and women across the Earth. They answered the first, tenuous questions that came when those hearts were no longer content to be captives of the social mind.

They took a million hands and led people back to the path toward home, then bid them a love-filled good-bye. Like rescuers in the black night on a stormy sea, they plucked people out of their ignorance and set them on a course for shore. Then they would dive back into the density of Earth to answer the call of another who cried for help in the darkness.

Continuing to travel, I received the message of the "Healers." All across the Earth, they held hearts in their hands the way the boy-child had held mine. They spoke to Adams everywhere, giving them strength and courage to continue, even when the social mind battered and betrayed him again and again. They mended the assaults of density upon people's connection to the third spirit. They sent hope into the hearts of people everywhere.

We passed the "Community of the Line," theirs a warrior task in the lifetimes. They drove back the darkness, keeping Earth and its beings safe from all that was not of the infinite heart. And they never seemed to grow tired. Their purpose relied on an unwavering heart, an endless supply of courage, and the ability to discern what is from what seems to be.

Another soul community's music met my nonexistent ears, and I knew they were of the "Consciousness of Christ." Their lifetimes were spent living, breathing, and carrying the true message of His name's work. They were conduits for the truth of what a lifetime on Earth truly means, and the reality of the soul that surrounds us. They wept for the destruction wrought on Earth in the name of Christ.

I heard, "Whenever two or more are called in my name, there I will be as well." And I understood the meaning for the first time. Wherever the first and second spirit are spun forth, there the love and guidance of the soul will be as well. I called to them, and they answered with indescribable compassion.

We approached another group, and I heard terrible wailing and weeping. I knew these were "Gaia's People." They moved across the Earth, trying to protect her creatures, repair her skin, cleanse her body. As they worked, density followed them like bitter black tar, encasing and suffocating every living thing. Still they worked, their hearts melting away the blackness wherever they could. And Gaia called them forth to Earth in groups, knowing their work must be done en masse. The time had long passed when a single life could make a difference all on its own.

In the midst of the cries, I saw incredible beauty in the faces their Adams had created. They were the First People all across the Earth; brown, red, yellow, black, and white. They rode the across the plains on pounding hoofs, ran through rain forests on powerful legs, nurtured forth Gaia's bounty and lived only for her. Drums called their warrior hearts forward, deep and resonant, ever willing to beat back the darkness of density, even as the war seemed lost.

Going on, I heard the "Community of Joseph." They were quiet, willing companions for all those in service to humanity. Strength and certainty of purpose radiated outward from them. I knew they had been present in all times when Earth's people had moved forward in understanding the soul. Yet they were seldom noticed, for theirs was a life of silent dedication.

Farther on, I saw the returning place for those whose life on Earth was now over. Astonished, I saw that the great love and powerful light that people reported seeing when they left their bodies at death was that of their own soul. The energy directed from the soul to sustain the lifetime condensed into a wondrous tunnel. As the soul absorbed the information gathered by the personality over its lifetime, images of people it had known were released. Events of the lifetime were reviewed by the soul as the personality made its journey home into the light. Immense, unwavering love poured from the soul as it welcomed its prodigal personality home.

I saw those souls draw their first and second spirits back into themselves, gleaning experiences that were essential to their evolution. They greeted density-battered hearts with love of an intensity never known inside the capsule of the social mind. I watched multitudes of people drift upward into the embrace of their souls. I saw their relief, their jubilation as they finally knew the truth that had never changed. For there had never been any reason to fear death. It was truly a glorious reunion. With a burst of joy, love swept into limitless ecstasy and the personality disappeared into the light of the soul.

A pathway of translucent ultraviolet light appeared before me. My heart began to vibrate, resonating with a spectacular sound . . . the song of forever. Fountains of blue and silver sparks flew outward in all directions, and an intoxicating melody called me into itself. Drawn forward, I knew what I had thought was heaven had only been the beginning.

A place appeared before me where all souls were in glorious communion with one another. In one ecstatic dance of love, they turned together in service to all souls below them. This place was beyond any heaven I had ever dreamed of. There was no angry God here, no judge, no punishment.

The souls moved together and yet were still somehow individual. They looked into one another's eyes and found an endless well of love. Their work was powerful. Each one directed profound concern toward the souls in the region we had just left. Their love rained down on all the communities and strengthened them. They sang without ceasing, propelling those souls toward their own evolution.

From this place, some still created lifetimes upon the Earth. Whenever a particular soul's work was important for the care of Gaia, or the advancement of consciousness, they would accompany that soul until it grew strong enough to fulfill its purpose alone. Then they bid good-bye, and the energies went back into the lap of the soul so it could spin forth another lifetime, another escort for another being. It seemed that members of the second heaven had more than one vehicle on the Earth at once.

Their energies were too powerful, their work too important to the evolution of all to wait for one life to return home.

My heart grew until it crossed the horizons of infinity. There I was surrounded with a blinding light from still another heaven. Waves of gold rolled in all directions, propelled by a deep, steady throb that swallowed my being. Here, souls were no longer separated, but were one boundless heart. Without ceasing, they gave glorious life to all the souls in the first and second heavens. By doing so, they gave life to all those on Earth.

The remaining solidified energy that bound my individual identity began to splinter. Finally, breaking into a thousand shards of light, they sent themselves out into forever. Then, there was no more separation, no more longing, no more thinking— nothing but love, an ecstatic, pure, powerful love.

And there in our arms, so tired, so afraid for her children, our sister Gaia was held. She was nursed on splendid waves of golden light; she was adored, and kept alive. The oceans were her blood, the rivers and streams her arteries, delivering nutrients throughout her body. And her hair, the magnificent trees blowing in the wind . . . her breath, the clouds in the sky.

All around her, we sang our love and gave our encouragement. "Do not give up on them, our sister. Some are beginning to see. Perhaps soon your burden will be lifted."

She shuddered with grief and called to us, "Please help them to see. They do not know what they do."

Our waves of translucent gold rose and fell beneath her body. She sighed softly and held her creatures to her breast. So many of them were too weak to drink, no longer able to take her nourishment, and they fell forever away. Her tears followed them out into infinity.

Here was the place from which humanity had fallen so long ago. All the souls of mankind were needed to make this heaven complete. We sent forth a deep yearning, and our arms stretched out to all who remained below in the other heavens. The mighty heart cried for those who were lost, like a mother cries for her child in the darkness. For a million years, the cries had gone out.

Gaia had willingly left this place and put herself into exile, ripped away from the body of the whole. She went to sustain those souls who were lost. She provided a way for them to return home.

And still we created the undulating rhythm with Gaia in our arms, pushing love through her body, praying for mercy, offering hope and nourishment from upper heaven.

Even beyond this beyond the beyond place, there was something else. We could sense infinite life breathing, an infinite heart beating, forever sending itself outward and bringing us back again. A voice called to us; its glorious sound sped along the strands of light that made up our being, infusing us with rapture and a boundless determination. Gaia's head lifted with joy, and we knew there was a second chance for humanity, perhaps only one more opportunity before Gaia's body gave out.

Suddenly, I knew what was wished of me.

◖ THIRTY-ONE ◗

It seemed I had been falling for a very long time. Wafting downward on a timeless wind, I descended through the three heavens, past countless glorious souls. Their eyes were everywhere, clear blue like a perfect summer sky, radiating love and eternal compassion.

Borne on the currents of love, my own soul joined with me and I watched it spin the body of "Karen" again. My awareness of that person and her lifetime came back fully. I began to weep, knowing I must go back and rejoin my destiny on Earth. Again I heard, "Do not be afraid, I am with you always."

Like a comet going across the night sky, light streamed from me in all directions, and my heart reentered the body of Karen. It seemed like a tiny space, a small vehicle to live in for the next decades on Earth.

Gaia reached up with enormous arms and caught me. I rested against her heart while love as powerful as all her seas surrounded me. I heard her whisper a willingness to sustain my life. But I had the responsibility to remember everything I had seen.

My soul spoke again. "Karen, you must go forth into the Earthtime and help the others remember. The hope for all humanity is for each person to remember who he or she really is."

The space grew tighter and tighter, and my vision began to eclipse until I could only see with my physical eyes. Now I was like a creature caught in a box, only able to see through a crack in the seam.

"Do not identify with the body." I heard the voice of my soul. "You can continue to see and know. You do not have to obey your senses. Remember, Karen. You must remember."

Then I wasn't trapped anymore, but continued to approach the surface of Earth with my ability to see beyond my senses.

There I was, suddenly standing again on firm ground, but it was no longer static and dead. I could feel Gaia breathing. I could hear her heart beating in harmony with mine. I could see all the trees around me, the birds flying by, the buzzing bee. They were all Gaia, different expressions of the same love. And when I looked at my surroundings, everything pulsed and hummed together, a living, breathing mosaic of love.

I moved my body slowly, feeling unfamiliar with this vehicle. My own heart turned rapidly, shooting light out all around me. I knew I could never run out of that melodious energy, unless I forgot and clogged up its capacity to receive from its maker.

Light flowed from every surface of my body, a panoply of violet, pink, subtle orange, and blue. I smiled with delight when a passing butterfly felt welcome to land on my arm. I remembered that the little black bug was my personality self, but the wings, the colored expanse of beauty . . . that was my soul. Those wings vibrated softly. The colors shimmered as she flew off, carried high on a gentle wind.

I looked around, trying to determine where I might be on the Earth. I recognized Boise once again. Off in the distance I could see Daniel, walking toward me. Closer now, he kicked the dirt with his high-tops like any other little kid. He grinned happily and called, "Hi, Karen!" as though nothing unusual had happened.

Looking at him with new eyes, I could see his heart wheel

spinning with brilliant silver light. My own heart continued to expand, now with gratitude, and with the beginnings of either ecstasy or hysteria. Whatever it was, I had no hope of controlling it. I choked out a question to which I already had the answer. "Daniel, I did it, didn't I? It wasn't a dream. I was there, wasn't I?"

"Yep," he said with gentle appreciation of my accomplishment.

Falling over backward can be a wonderful thing. It completely removes any pretense of being all right. You are free at that point to come completely unglued. I didn't really know what that meant, but I was tired of trying to prevent it. I was just going to lose it, fall apart, scream, cry, talk gibberish, and be done with it. But nothing happened. I let go and nothing happened. To be sure, I was lying flat on my back, but that didn't seem to be particularly significant.

"Daniel?" I called out weakly. "Are you there?" Giant black basketballs floated in front of me, obscuring my vision.

Somewhere to my left, Daniel's voice sounded like it was under water. "Of course, where else would I be?"

"Don't leave me, okay?"

"Okey dokey." The child's phrase lingered in my mind like an old melody, comforting and familiar.

Tears ran down my face. And I finally asked, "Why me? Why did you show me?"

"Why not you?" he replied simply.

"Well, I guess I believe there are people who would be more worthy than I am . . ."

Daniel began laughing so hard he could scarcely breathe. Taking in a huge gulp of air, he soon used it up in another round of hysterical giggling. He managed to send out a few words. "Oh, Karen! Do you try to be so silly, or do you just do it naturally?"

"Wait a minute! What's so funny?" My feelings were hurt. Admitting there may be others in the world who are better people than you are is a difficult thing to do. I certainly had not expected to be laughed at.

Nonetheless, the child was howling. "It's just that after seeing everything, it seems so funny you would still think about who's better and who's not!"

I looked at him in dismay, and he suddenly stopped laughing. "For heaven's sake, Karen, that's what it's all about . . . getting over the idea that somebody else deserves to know more about spirit! We want all of you to see and know firsthand, just like you were meant to. That's the whole point!"

He gazed at me with a new compassion. "Don't you know by now that you are all so loved? You are all worthy of knowing the truth. Your soul waits to take you into its arms, it doesn't measure whether you deserve it or not. When you feel unworthy, it grieves for your suffering and constantly sings its love. But you see, your own bitter voice of condemnation drowns out that sweet sound."

The words softened what remained of my stubbornness, and I began to cry again. He reached out his hands, and I took hold of them with the trust of a child determined not to let go. Bringing my head to rest against his little chest, I heard him whisper, "Oh, Karen, just remember who you really are."

I closed my eyes and thought of all I had seen. I knew now where I had come from and what surrounded me in each moment of my life. My soul was not "out there," or "up there," it was right here with me. It had been here all along. I had turned my back on the boundless acceptance of my own soul. I had never fallen short of being worthy to receive its love—it came without interruption. I had blocked myself off from that wellspring.

But I could no longer afford to become lost. I now knew

firsthand what only a few others had ever seen. I knew what was possible for all human beings.

Rousing myself, I said softly, "You know, I always thought there was one heaven and everybody would go there at death. At least that's what I thought when I believed in heaven at all." I hadn't really believed we would be wearing white robes and playing harps, which had always sounded like an awful waste of time. But I had thought there was only a single place.

"Well," he said matter-of-factly, "there is more than one. And in the first heaven, souls are still spinning lifetimes so they can gather information and experiences that will help them evolve." He was pulling blades of grass from the bottom of his shoe.

But I was riveted to our conversation, "Do you mean they're kind of climbing toward the higher heavens?"

"Yep. Wouldn't have to, except they all got so lost in the first place. Like I already told you." He gave up and pulled his shoe off. Banging it on the ground, he pounded away the remaining grass.

I had many friends who believed that the soul was perfection itself, and that our task was to grow enough to be able to consult that soul for the answers in life. But if our souls were already complete, why would we continue to need lifetimes? In the soul's need to evolve, and our role in helping it, for the first time I had an explanation that made sense!

"So they're continuing to drop their density and regain the lightness, the purity to return all the way home?"

"Yep."

A surge of excitement rose within me. "That's why it's so important that we remember who we are! We need to do that so that we can liberate ourselves from the social mind and help Gaia. But our souls rely on what we bring them in order to advance. What good are we to them if we're just thrashing around in the capsule?"

He smiled with pleasure as I grasped the reality of my own true importance. "Well, all experience is valuable. But you can certainly help a whole lot more if you're connected to the soul you're supposed to help. How else can you figure out your life purpose?"

"Life purpose?" I had heard people talk about this many times. It seemed that we were all searching for something that would help us make sense out of what we were doing on Earth. After all, life in the capsule didn't have anything at all to offer. Intuitively, we had always known that.

"See, most of you on the Earth belong to one of the communities. Of course, everything is always free will, and you can do whatever you want to do. But your life will be more valuable and go a lot better if what you do is in agreement with your soul community."

Excitedly I said, "I saw how the souls were spinning lifetimes using some kind of energy they got from their communities. That purpose is an integral part of who we are on Earth, isn't it?"

"Yep." He knew I had much more to ask.

"Daniel, this has tremendous implications! Knowing how we should serve our soul, and knowing what community our soul comes from, could answer an awful lot of questions." I took a deep breath and felt immense relief inside. For my whole life, I had been asking what the point of being here might be.

"That's why when people try to do stuff apart from their soul, it never works out very well. There's a whole lot of people who are living in ways that have nothing to do with their deepest purpose. It makes for a lot of confusion and frustration, and an endless searching for meaning."

"I know. I know. That's what most of my work as a counselor has been about. I've tried hard to help people find their true identity, and some meaning in life. But I had no idea!"

He began to giggle. "I know about those funny tests psychologists give people. You know, the ones that try to help them figure out what they should be doing!" He was laughing uproariously. "What a goofy thing to do!"

"Daniel, that's the best we had. None of us knew about communities or any of what I just saw!" A flurry of questions flew up in my mind. "And why are there soul communities? And how many communities are there? Does each person's soul stay in one community forever? How does the soul residing in a community affect a person's lifetime on Earth?" I paused to take a gulp of air.

"Karen, slow down!" Daniel giggled. "You sure have a lot of questions."

"Of course I have a lot of questions! This is so important. My God, do you know how much time we spend trying to figure out what we're supposed to be doing with our lives?"

"Yep," he said, suddenly somber. "An awful lot of mistakes get made."

"Well . . ." I was waiting for my answers. "Tell me about those communities, Daniel. Tell me more."

"Okay," he said, pausing just long enough to pique my interest even more. "There are seven of them, but you're only ready to know about six. "

Not waiting for me to protest, Daniel went on. "Spiritual communities are communities of purpose, not of place. Each community provides a series of lessons for the soul. Each soul will pass through all of the communities in the course of its process of development. The soul doesn't go through different communities in one lifetime, but in a series of lifetimes. Your current lifetime is supposed to be an expression of the community your soul is connected with."

"So," I interrupted excitedly, "if we know what community our soul is in, we have some very big clues about what direction our life should go."

"Yep," he replied. "If you make your life choices so that they match up with your soul's spiritual community, you give your soul exactly what it needs to grow."

"And each soul community is very different?" I asked. "I mean, the lessons a particular soul needs are very specific?"

"Very different. And characteristics found in that community were woven into your being when you were created. This special pattern exists outside your ordinary awareness, but it continually insists that you move in the direction determined by your soul's community. The information buried deep in your core sends up directions about which job you should do, what relationships you should seek out, and how you should spend your time on Earth."

There was such hope for all of us contained in the information about spiritual communities. We had searched and floundered, trying to follow what the social mind told us. Unless we fell into something that was consistent with our soul community, our hit-or-miss approach only yielded frustration, problematic relationships, and feelings of emptiness. If we knew about our soul community, we would no longer be living blindly, we would have essential guidelines to go by.

Daniel continued. "But the more density the personality clogs itself up with, the more difficult it is for that important instruction from your community to seep through . . . what was meant to have spiritual purpose ends up serving the social mind."

I choked at the thought of that mean little woman inside me gaining control over one more thing that was meant to be a gift from my soul. The more information I could gain, the harder it would be for that social mind to creep in and steal what was rightfully mine. "Daniel, can you tell me about each community? I saw them and heard them, but I want more."

"Well, let's look at the First Step community," he replied cheerily. "The role of this community is to help others to take their first steps on the spiritual path. At the soul level, there's no ego about that. Nobody feels like they're more advanced than anyone else. These souls simply volunteer to go into the density of Earth to do a specific job. They shine a light in the middle of the thick, dense energy so that others can find the path that leads back home."

"That sounds wonderful, Daniel." I thought for a moment and then asked, "How could I recognize a First Step person . . . I mean, one who is in alignment with his or her soul's community purpose?"

"They're not very hard to see! They're . . . well they're . . . intense, that's it! They always need to find meaning in whatever they do. There is no such thing as just wandering through life for them."

I interrupted. "Are these the people who are incredibly single-minded about whatever they are trying to accomplish? The ones who can be pretty unwilling to listen to the suggestions and advice of others?"

"That's right," he said. "More than any other community, these people must have freedom. They don't like being told what to do or how to do it. But they're really brave! If there's a project to be organized, a goal to be reached, a plan to be developed, they're the first ones to step forward."

"I've known lots of people like that, Daniel," I broke in. "If you put them in a situation where rules dominate, they will challenge the rules, reinvent them, ask why they are in place and develop new ways to do the task at hand!"

"Yep," he said, a note of clear appreciation in his voice. "First Step people are really searching to satisfy a need deep inside. Their very reason for being on Earth is spiritually based. Until they find a way to act on their purpose, they put a fiery effort into a job only to be left with an empty feeling inside. So they're restless in jobs and relationships, always seeking their true reason for being here."

"But you said the social mind distorts the instructions from our soul's community. If that happens with a First Step person, what would he or she be like?"

"Well, they'd get really unhappy with themselves and with life itself. They'd end up running around, changing jobs and relationships, moving to different places, 'without any good reason.' The social mind tells them they are being flighty or unreasonable, but it only makes the First Step person more determined to live life in his or her own way."

"It sounds like they can get pretty desperate." I was thinking of clients I had seen who were probably lost First Step members.

"Yep." The child nodded solemnly. "The key to inner peace for the First Stepper is to find meaningful work with a spiritual purpose. If they don't know to create that for themselves, they feel like they're just wasting their time on Earth."

"I guess they could get really depressed."

"Not really," he answered with a grin. "First Steppers don't have the patience to sit around being depressed. Instead, they run around and around stabbing at different projects, relationships and jobs, endlessly seeking the reason they are alive."

I shook my head and asked, "Daniel . . . why haven't we known about spiritual communities all this time?"

"Just another thing lost in the confusion," he answered. "Want to know about another community?" he said brightly.

"Of course I do."

"Well, how about the Line community? I know you don't understand yet, but the universe isn't all good. Somebody has to maintain the line between darkness and light. The Line community protects all the other communities."

"Everything isn't all good?" I squeaked. I didn't feel ready to hear more information about that yet.

"Nope," the little boy answered cryptically. Then he went on with his explanation. "At the personality level, concern over separating one kind of energy from another can make a person who is overly cautious. Because their soul has seen the consequences of not watching carefully for the darkness, the personality feels a strong mission to protect other people."

I had no trouble thinking of people who were probably Line community members. Brimming with integrity and loyalty, they were fierce warriors, the last to give up in any conflict. They had incredible endurance, staying with anything important well beyond others who grew discouraged. But they could also be very controlling.

"I bet this kind of personality is often seen as black and white in their thoughts and actions. Sometimes they don't have much flexibility."

"Well, they don't really want to control anybody. It's just that they think keeping other people within certain boundaries is the key to keeping them safe. They look for possible dangers in everything. That can be very frustrating to the members of other communities who are trying to open up and explore new things. If a Line member is part of a group, they will be the 'wait a minute, let's consider this carefully' voice. This can dampen the enthusiasm of others who are creatively pushing forward with a new idea."

I shook my head. "Isn't it practically impossible to find spirit if you can't open up?"

He nodded sadly. "They have the hardest time connecting with their own souls. Letting go feels dangerous. Staying on the well-worn path feels safe. But this lack of connection to their souls is a tragedy for them and hard for everybody around them. See, they have an unbelievable talent for knowing who can be trusted. But when they get too closed off from spirit, their true ability gets amplified into a lack of trust for anything or anyone unknown."

"They can seem like people with no interest in spirit at all!"

"But see," Daniel said quietly, "if you look at this group carefully, they have a true concern that others will get hurt, either emotionally or physically. They are the people who try to protect everyone around them from dangerous energies only they are able to see."

"So, they are the protectors of family, property, animals—anything they regard as being within their field of concern!" I immediately thought of a particular friend. I had always known he would be the first person to call if anything went really wrong. Whenever I was near him, I felt safe.

"Yep," the little boy said.

"Daniel, I'm getting it! I can see how people I know fit into these communities. It really does help me to understand them."

He smiled, waiting for my next round of questions. I thought for a minute and remembered the passion I had seen in the members of the Gaia community. "The souls concerned with Gaia . . . what a job they have cut out for them!"

"Oh, Karen, you're just starting to understand," he said sadly. "The first souls on Earth were all members of the Gaia community. First People everywhere lived in intimate contact with their mother. She generously offered her body so they could grow. Humanity loved and cared for her as a living being. Hers was the voice and heart that was to remain constant. But much of humanity has forgotten Gaia. Earth is seen by most of your world as a piece of rock. Her creatures are seen as possessions, and the sky and water have become dumping grounds. Still, Gaia continues to try to give."

"We don't even realize that Earth is someone's body!" I cried.

"No you don't. Now, Gaia members can be found outside native cultures around the globe. In cities and natural areas, these souls manifest bodies and personalities that reflect the concerns of Gaia. They love natural surroundings, even a tiny city park. If a Gaia member is kept away from nature, she becomes anxious, depressed and even physically ill. They have a passionate concern for animals, for every plant and member of the ecological system."

"I guess they have to get pretty militant about that," I interrupted. "The more Gaia is harmed, the more passionate they must be about saving her." I thought about organizations like Greenpeace, People for the Ethical Treatment of Animals, and Earth First. Their methods had always seemed extreme. But the life work of the members of the Gaia community was to save her.

Daniel was nodding. "They have to overcome all of the destruction. They are trying hard to bring awareness of Gaia's existence, and gratitude for her sacrifices, back into the emotional vocabulary of humanity."

"A very big job," I said somberly. "I guess we don't treat Gaia community people much better than we treat her."

"No," he answered. "The Gaia person is often treated with the same lack of respect with which most people treat Gaia." Smiling a little, he added, "They can seem kind of strange. They usually don't care about fashion or modern conveniences. Such things seem trivial compared to Gaia's beauty and resources. And they aren't interested in conforming to schedules or social styles. They can be at odds with your modern world. Earth's natural rhythms tell them when and how to do things. Their personality can be irritating to those caught up in the social mind."

"Members of the First Step community probably have a hard time with them. They are busy trying to achieve specific goals while the Gaia people move at a different pace."

"It can be really hard for them," he agreed. "Separated from their way of life by society's worship of the social mind, Gaia members can wander lost and depressed. When it's a beautiful day, they just want to be outside, smelling the Earth, watching the dance of nature, and feeding the birds. They can be easily distracted by anything of natural beauty, or the needs of an animal or child. By the standards of the social mind, the Gaia person is somebody who doesn't care about anything really important."

"I bet they struggle with low self-esteem," I ventured. "If we don't see Gaia as important, how can we see anyone in rhythm with her as important?"

"Yep. They can take a long time to find the right place for themselves. They are often changing course in their education and in their work lives. If other people try to push them in a particular direction, Gaia people will often get really depressed, and the person who is trying to change them gets really frustrated."

I thought of a client from a few years back. I remembered how his teeth had clenched when he told me, "My son finally got a wonderful job working for the post office. What did he do? He insisted on a month off so he can throw himself in front of a logging truck to save some damned owl." But to that man's son, the owl was Gaia herself. His soul was sending him a relentless message to protect her, not keep a job that was meaningless to him.

"And then there's the Community of Joseph," Daniel broke in. "That's a harder one to explain. But they're awfully important."

"Try, Daniel," I said urgently.

"Well, they're the people who help others who are trying hard to create spiritual change on the Earth. A lot of the time, nobody notices or appreciates them. But without their quiet strength and support, the others couldn't do their difficult work."

"That's an odd name," I interjected. "Where does it come from? What does it mean?"

"We got it from one of the greatest examples of this community," he said.

"Joseph . . . well, the most famous Joseph I know is the father of Jesus."

"Right!" Daniel grinned. "He's a perfect example, kind of mysterious. Nobody pays much attention to him, except to mention he was by Mary's side."

"He does kind of disappear in the accounts of Jesus' life," I agreed.

"That's because people in this community are always in the background. When they're not needed anymore, they go find somebody else to help."

"They do sound unique," I mused.

"The souls in this community are at a more advanced level of spiritual development. That higher state of evolution lends them special insight about what has to be fixed in order for humanity to progress. Their personalities are uninterested in the concerns of social mind. So they are able to make what others consider enormous sacrifices in service to spiritual work. But they don't see it as sacrifice. What could be more important than waking people up to their true identity and purpose?"

"But," I interrupted, "you said they help others who are doing spiritual work. Isn't that a little codependent? Can't the people from the Community of Joseph just do the work?"

"No," he said passionately. "It isn't that Joseph people are hiding behind a stronger person. They aren't doormats. Their work is active, dedicated, and unwavering. They know what must be done and offer a steadying energy to those who must do it."

"What do they do, exactly?"

"Well, they are always in the inner circle of those who do important spiritual work. Standing in the background, they take in what goes on, then offer their balanced and beautiful encouragement and support. They quietly make sure their star stays focused, healthy, and filled with optimism."

He continued. "They have an incredible belief in humanity's ability to grow beyond its tragic state of confusion. Joseph people quietly rejoice when spiritual growth occurs on a personal or planetary level. It's like they've been standing for a long time at the top of a mountain and they're really, really happy when someone else makes a successful climb."

"Can density interfere with their personality selves like it can with those who belong to other communities?" I wanted to make sure I could recognize a Joseph community person if I ran into him.

Daniel heaved a sad sigh. "When they get clogged up with density, they're truly tragic people. They have to fall long and hard to forget the lessons they have learned in their progress to higher evolution. But the social mind is so powerful that it can even interfere with those on Earth from this community."

"That does sound sad," I replied. "What happens to them?"

"They get caught in abusive relationships a lot. Because they're able to see the spiritual beauty in everyone, they'll put up with awful behavior from other people far longer than members of other communities would."

I was afraid to ask for clarification about the next community. Carefully, I ventured my delicate question. "What about the Consciousness of Christ community, Daniel? Did they get horribly confused along the way? I mean, well . . . Jesus' message got awfully mixed up."

"No, no," he shouted. "It's not their fault at all! Well, just look!"

◖ THIRTY-TWO ◗

Suddenly somewhere else, I frantically looked around for a clue about where I might be. Caught in the crevice between two small sand dunes, I stumbled to my feet. Daniel was nowhere to be seen. The sun blazed unforgivingly.

Wiping away the sweat that had already sprung from my brow, I climbed up the little hill, deep scorching sand grabbing at my feet. A wider view offered no further information. Melting into the distance, the horizon gently rose and fell with the heat.

"Daniel!" I cried. "Where am I? Why did you send me out here?" The silence of the barren desert mocked my desperation. I tried to decide which direction to walk. "Daniel! Where do I go? What do you want me to do?" Fear found only anger to embrace, and I moved forward, hands attempting to shield me from the sun.

Off in the distance, a rumbling sound emerged from the emptiness. Soon it escalated into a distinct, pounding rhythm. It sounded oddly familiar.

As I looked frantically in the direction of the sound, colors began to appear—blue, red, silver. Was that a flag? People! People on horseback! My heart swelled with gratitude, and I began to wave wildly, hoping for rescue.

As the people grew closer, my mind screamed in confusion. This can't be! "Oh, no . . . no. Daniel!"

Sun glaring from their armor, the men pounded toward me.

Enraged, they bore down on me, carrying their bright blue flag with fiery certainty. The red symbol emblazoned upon it held no mystery . . . the cross! My God . . . "Daniel!"

Could it be? Had he really sent me to face these warriors alone? These men were from another time. There could only be one explanation. I had to be in the Holy Land, and this must be the time of the Crusades. "Daniel! Why? Please! Help me!"

Swords unsheathed, the men were now only ten feet away. I screamed in agony at my impending fate. "Please! Please! I mean you no harm. I'm here by accident! Please!"

"Infidel! God-cursed pagan! Be gone from this world!" The warrior roared his condemnation, and I prepared for my end. It was so unfair, so profoundly wrong. But his pale blue eyes blazed with ferocious intent. That cross . . . my God, I thought, don't you understand what that cross really means?

Rigid with dread, I could do nothing but wait for death. "Daniel, why? Oh God, why?"

Swiftly taken by unseen arms, I found myself abruptly in another place. The warriors were gone. And I was still alive. "Where am I?" I whispered through a sandpaper throat. "Daniel?"

Then I heard the voices screaming—mocking, violent, angry. "Burn her! Burn the witch!" Crowds swarmed around me, pushing my quivering body toward a tangle of brush.

"Please! Please! I'm here by accident. I'm not who you think I am!"

"Burn the witch!" Cold, glittering, eyes came close to mine. A gaunt white hand clutched a shimmering piece of gold. "Kiss this symbol of our Lord and hope to find your way out of your punishment in hell," its owner rasped.

The cross! My God . . . don't you know what that really means? "Please! Please! I'm not who you think I am!"

Swept upward, I was propelled into yet another time. Looking around, gratefully I recognized contemporary surroundings. "Daniel! Am I back in Boise? Where are you?"

Men and women sat together around a battered oak table. There was intense anger in this place. Their words were sharp like shards of glass. Their faces burned with peculiar intensity.

"We must fight to regain this country for God," one man growled. "Our Lord will ignite us with courage to do our work."

As I watched them carefully, it was clear they could not see me. Softly, I walked around their table, anxious to discover what they were planning. "They deserve what they get!" a woman said bitterly. "Our Bible makes it clear. Those who are not for God are to be seen as enemies."

Slowly, a short, round man raised his head and whispered, "But can it truly be right to do these things?"

"In the name of Jesus, we can only be right!" the woman snarled.

Shooting to his feet, the oldest man slammed his hand on the table. When he pulled his hand away, I could see an enormous wooden cross left behind. "We will do what we must!" he bellowed. "We are the soldiers of God's will!"

Oh, I cried. Don't you know what that cross truly means? Please stop your violence! Stop!

"They can't hear you." The familiar small voice was filled with grief. "We keep trying to reach them, but they never listen."

"Daniel?" I couldn't see him, but we had left the angry people behind.

Now I was spiraling rapidly upward. Silver, blue, and gold flew past in a flurry of sparkling beauty. The tears of a thousand souls washed away my pain, and I was magically transported back into the realms of heaven.

ᘒ THIRTY-THREE ᘒ

Soft hands caressed my being, and a sweet song wound its way through my heart.

"Peace be with you, and know that we are God."

Carried aloft on a gentle breeze, I let myself go, knowing I was home again.

"Peace be with you, and know that we are."

Whispering fingers swept over my body, and delicate kisses fluttered across my skin.

"Peace be with you, and know."

Sweet, boundless love washed over me as waves of comfort replaced all fear.

"Peace be with you."

Radiant eyes gazed into mine and there . . . ah, there I found such glory.

"Peace."

Luminous beings held me in their arms, stroking my heart and sending exquisite rushes of indescribable joy throughout my consciousness.

Again, in the midst of translucent, shimmering light, my heart turned rapidly with ecstatic, limitless energy. All around me, love and compassion flowed in tangible form, fountains of magnificent light came in sparkling profusion, their destination my heart.

"Our message is not of hate and violence," they murmured.

"For so long, we have only tried to awaken humanity to the reality of its being. You are pure love. That is how we have made you. That is what you are."

"The Christ community," I whispered. "That is where I am." I had no need to question, the love I was feeling so clearly could only come from them.

Transparent, glimmering hands continued their soothing caresses. "The message of Christ has been so terribly distorted. We have only given humanity instruction about density and the need to return to the energies of the soul. But this has been translated into dogma and destruction."

The voices softly continued. "The Consciousness of Christ has little to do with churches or theology. In fact, it has little to do with Christianity as followed by much of the world. Christ consciousness can be found in people who have never heard of Jesus, or of the church produced in his name."

"Oh." I closed my eyes to accept their comfort. "There have been some terrible mistakes."

"The energy of our community can be found in those who know that man is not what he appears to be—limited, often violent, power-hungry, and confused. The message of Christ is lived out by those who go beyond personality and toward the soul that surrounds them every day. We are not judgmental or punitive. Can you not feel that we only know unconditional and absolute love for the beings we have created?"

"And your purpose is only to bring us home," I murmured, content to remain forever in their arms.

"For two thousand years, the Christ community has been the leading community on the Earth. We were charged with awakening humanity to the spiritual reality of its existence. All over the Earth, we have sought to teach people how to reach their souls, how to drop their density and bring the energies of love into everyday life. It did not matter whether they did this work in the name of Jesus or another teacher. Our message was the same."

"Oh," I said softly, tears beginning to fall. "Instead of accepting the help, learning to grow, and being open to love, humanity has reacted with violence. We killed your teacher so early in his life."

"Indeed. And other teachers have been relentlessly persecuted. Institutions of power have destroyed cultures around the world, all under the guise of saving souls. Even the cross has lost its original meaning and become only the macabre representation of an execution."

"How have you tried to do your work?" I asked without words.

"We work by example. We use our own subtle energy, seeking only to remind humanity about who you really are, spiritually created beings with a distinct purpose on Earth. You must learn to destroy only density and the social mind, not each other."

"The Bible . . ." I ventured. "That didn't come from you?"

"Oh, no," the voices whispered. "People created it out of misunderstanding of our true message. It became only a document of density, something filled with the confusion and ignorance of those separated from the soul. But people around the world follow this document as absolute truth. The Bible has done little more than produce more density."

Clearly, a clerical collar or grand church didn't automatically reveal true affiliation with this loving group. "How can I recognize a true Christ community member on Earth?"

A gentle laugh preceded the reply. "Often he or she is not affiliated with a religious institution, although some do work for reform within those institutions. Offering unconditional love, their speech is free of blame or attempts to control anyone. Instead, they understand that the soul's energies can only be brought into the Earthtime by melting away density and accepting spiritual reality. This cannot be accomplished by hurting others, but rather by example, patience, and unsurpassed gentleness."

This had nothing to do with pounding the pulpit or frightening people with divine punishment.

"An encounter with a true Christ community member leaves you with the rare feeling of total acceptance. Their faces often radiate a kind of love that has nothing to do with what you may have accomplished, what you look like, what culture you belong to. Theirs is often a life spent in service to others, building institutions that awaken humanity to spiritual truth.

"True members call out constantly for a return to love, a return to the soul. They may be accused of being too passive and accepting, appearing to lack the strength to compete in the modern world. But the Christ community member can show an intense endurance and tenacity toward those things that serve to reunite humanity with the soul. Their lack of interest in competition results from an awareness that pitting one person against another only creates separation, the opposite of the love-filled energies of the soul."

Surely, they did not try to do their work alone. "Do the other communities help you?"

"All communities have humanity's reawakening as their ultimate service. But the social mind distorts the instruction from the soul. The spiritual violence in your world is perpetrated by those of great confusion and density. Sometimes those people are lost members of the Christ community, and sometimes they are confused members of other communities."

I considered what I had learned about the other communities. "The Line community, all of their concern for safety and protection . . . if the social mind gets its hands on that and plays it out—religious dogma, threats of eternal damnation, that's what happens, isn't it?"

"Often, confused members of the Line community use the name of Christ to justify their attempts to protect others from darkness. This can result in intense efforts to keep others inside the lines of religious dogma, and even in fanatic groups dedicated to saving humanity from perceived evils, even pitting one group against another. The Jews and Native Americans were dehumanized for the purpose of extermination in the name of Christ. Many religious wars were created by misguided Line members."

The voices sighed. "Power, control, and judgment are all aspects of density, not of Christ. When religion is used to beat someone into submission, that is a sign of density, not of Christ."

"Don't give up on us," I cried softly. "Please, never give up."

"We shall never abandon you," they answered. "We have promised never to forsake you. But, soon, the Christ community will give way to the Healing community, who will try to help humankind."

Urged to open my eyes, I saw thousands of light-filled souls gathered together. In their midst, the spectacular body of Gaia turned and radiated enormous joy. Sweeping her up in gentle hands, they held her aloft. Mother, sister, lover, she was a priceless gift, almost ready to be offered to another community for their unique care.

Now that community appeared. Countless incandescent beings reached out with unwavering love. Their song wrapped around her exquisite body, offering encouragement and hope. They waited only for the right moment to receive her beauty.

"Soon," the Christ community sang back. "Soon the time will come."

I understood clearly that the time was fast approaching when members of the Healing community would bear the responsibility for helping humanity awaken to its spirituality. People were realizing that the old ways had not worked well for physical, emotional, or spiritual healing. Even now, streams of brilliant energy were being sent to Earth by the Healing community.

The Christ community had been overwhelmed by humanity's continued insistence on increasing its density. Gaia was profoundly weakened as a result of the social mind's growing strength.

Without words, the Healing community allowed me to understand that they would go straight into the human heart and try to cleanse it of all energies that were not of the soul.

The Christ community had offered extensive information and support dedicated to making humanity aware of the soul. But now, people were unable to contact the soul, even if they decided they wished to. This was a result of density blocking the natural pathway for communication with that soul. Unless the heart was cleared, we would be destined to search in vain for the voice of our ultimate lover.

I knew why we had been constantly exposed to harmful energies of others in our world. We had forgotten a unique and essential part of ourselves that cleanses those energies before they ever reach the heart. We had become garbage collectors for the energies of hurt, resentment, and anger sent out by those around us. It didn't matter whether those people voiced their feelings, they still sent out contaminating energies. Like a sponge, we had automatically absorbed those energies. We ended up with an increasingly burdened heart that could no longer find the soul.

The social mind would actively oppose the Healing community's work. For once an individual's heart was clean, he would no longer wish to submit to the control of the social mind, and that dangerous implant would cease to exist.

Healers would be found in many places. They would become leaders of nations who sought to create only peace. They would work at professions dedicated to easing humanity's pain. True Healers would know that a human being is an energy system, the spirit its creator. Healers would transform the painful energies contained within the field of the person and effect true liberation from the contamination within us. This would be accomplished with endless patience, unconditional acceptance, and radiating love.

By moving the energy within himself, the Healer could provide a vibration that the people around him could copy, and thus shift themselves back into a healthy balance. In effect, the Healer would create the specific energy conditions by which people could heal themselves. This community would soothe Adams, heal wounds, and teach us again about the hidden methods by which we could keep our hearts pure.

Looking out over the thousands of Healing community souls, I saw that each one carefully cupped a human heart in its hands. These hearts were not made of flesh and blood, but of magnificent, shimmering energy. Quietly, the hearts turned, radiating translucent colors like the wings of a dragonfly in the sun. So gently, each soul sang a divine melody of endless compassion and joy to the heart, causing it to spin even faster.

The Healing community would work to help people all over the Earth to awaken their hearts. Heart wheels would be cleansed, unclogged, and the energies of the soul could again find their way through the darkness of density.

I could see the glorious possibilities. "Oh, God, that can be a new beginning for Gaia, for all of Earth's people," I cried. "If we can get our hearts moving again, everything will change!"

Spectacular smiles swept across the Healing community, and their sparkling light increased with joy.

I basked in the warmth of those smiles, but then my enthusiasm suddenly was dampened. I looked out at them and saw their light decrease as they understood what I was thinking. "But the social mind . . . the social mind won't like that at all."

"No, it won't," they replied sadly.

"I can hear them now," I muttered in frustration. "Opening the heart is a ridiculous, sloppy, sentimental idea that doesn't have anything to do with reality."

"Tragically, that is true."

"And then they'll say, 'We can't afford to do that, it's too dangerous in today's world to be running around opening ourselves up to who knows what.' "

"Indeed," they sighed. "And what will you answer, Karen?"

The answer made its way up from my deepest being, "But you don't go outside into the world to do your work! It's all an inside job! It's not about cramming your philosophy down somebody's throat or spouting greeting-card sentimentality. It's about your taking responsibility to clear away your own density and making your own heart wheel spin. That way, you can bring a new kind of energy into the world—not a concept about energy, not a philosophy about love, but an actual, tangible force that can change the world!"

Again, the radiant light increased and the eyes shined with absolute love. I was hyperventilating. "This second chance . . . will we have help, like when Jesus came? Will there be a new teacher to help us?"

"Indeed."

Confusion found its way through my joy. "Is that what Jesus spoke of as the Second Coming?"

"Oh, no. His message was profoundly distorted."

Resting here in the arms of these glorious souls, I continued to receive the love that I knew was available for all of humanity. They would never abandon us! The idea that Jesus would appear to save his followers while God destroyed everyone else was tragically confused. There truly was no angry, punitive God. There never was an avenging God coming to get us.

"Just power and fear," the souls replied to my unasked questions. "In truth, Jesus did not say anything like that. He was simply reminding you that if you identify with your personality self, and the little capsule, someday your body will die, which looks like the absolute end of your life."

It was so elegantly simple. Jesus had tried only to tell us that physical life is short. The statement "The end of the world is at hand" related to us personally. Our bodies do not last very long. We all die.

"He was just reminding you how to avoid that sense of a terrible end. Learn to move your identity into the realm of the soul. We are right here. We are who you truly are and always will be. We never end, and we will always love you. It is you who walls yourself off from that. Do not stubbornly stay fixed inside the body and the personality, which end. Embrace yourself as something that exists forever."

I smiled at the beauty of this message. If we stayed in the capsule, only knowing the body and the personality, death would be a terribly frightening thing to face. But if we came out of our capsule and knew firsthand who and what we are, then there would be no end to fear.

Still, there was something from the Bible that bothered me. "What about Revelations?" I finally asked. "There is so much frightening information about the end of the world."

"It is only distorted information about what happens if you insist on remaining with the body after its death. The body will decompose, and if you are still identifying with it, much pain will come to you."

I took in a deep breath and tried to resolve my remaining concerns. "The concept of Jesus coming to save those who believe in him was all about telling us again to believe in our souls. Experience it, accept it, and know that it is the only way out of the tragedy when your world ends. The soul is the only part of you that lives in heaven, so that's the only way you will ever get there. Be your soul and live forever, or be your personality and body and suffer in your lifetime and at the end of that life."

"Indeed," the souls replied. "His message was quite simple."

Joy exploded within me. Like most of what I had learned today, this information was nowhere near what I had been taught to believe. Nobody had really known what to do with Revelations. In my church tradition, it was usually just ignored. But so many scholars had tried to figure out what this strange book really meant.

"Many keepers have terrified the people they were supposed to be helping," the souls said sadly. "Your keepers have made you fear God. In truth, there is nothing at all to fear."

I began to cry again, understanding how we had alienated ourselves from such incredible love.

"The Bible was changed so many times. Whenever those who sought power needed to confuse the people, they just changed the information. Study the myths of Greece and Rome, Persia, Egypt, and Palestine. Those stories found their way into Revelations."

For centuries, people had been terrified by the material in the last book of the Bible. I was aghast at the enormity of the deception. But I gathered myself and dared to ask another question. "Back to the help we're going to get. It won't be Jesus, will it?"

"No," they replied.

"Well, then who will it be? Will there be some kind of dramatic entrance? What should I look for?"

"You will know," the souls answered.

"I have no idea," I stammered. "I don't know how to tell . . ." But suddenly I was flooded with an amazing realization. Of course I would know! "My heart! I'll know because I have a different heart now! I'll hear my soul tell me when the second chance begins!"

Excitement shot through me like lightning. "This opportunity will be seen by all of us who develop our hearts! The eyes and ears of the body will be irrelevant, because this isn't something you see or hear. All those stories about trumpets and thunder, they aren't true at all!"

Softly, I heard, "Spirit is everywhere. But its energies are subtle. If you do not develop the capacity to perceive them, you will never experience them. If you do not experience them, how would you know of life in our realm?"

"The help that's coming could be standing right in front of us and we wouldn't see it!" I felt incredibly invigorated about the possibilities ahead. "People have to start doing their work! If they don't start unclogging their heart wheels, they won't know when this wonderful help comes. If we don't have a way to receive the message, it won't matter how powerful the being is who sends it."

I went on with overwhelming excitement. "Because Jesus didn't come to save us and this new teacher won't either. We have to do our own work. That's the bottom line, isn't it?"

"It has always been so, and always will be so."

"But we're never alone." It wasn't that we were abandoned and left adrift like some awful cosmic experiment, we were just stubbornly cutting ourselves off from what had surrounded us the whole time.

The souls sighed as one and replied, "Not unless you choose to be."

"I have to help!" I cried with a passion I never knew I had.

"I know what is wished of me. I have to help people to remember!"

"That is why we have called you," the souls sang out.

"But I'm just a therapist in Boise, Idaho. What can I do? How can I possibly do what you want me to?"

"You will have help," the souls replied. "You are not alone."

"You are always with me. But nobody knows about any of this. How will I convince anybody about what I have seen? Nobody will believe me! Choose someone else! I can't do it!" This was so incredibly important for humanity. I had seen and heard so much, but how in the world could I ever help others to understand?

The souls sang a sweet reply. "You must not try to convince anyone. It is not for you to convert or overcome anyone's beliefs. Simply tell them. Offer your experience, offer your love, offer endless compassion and enduring strength. Each must decide whether to follow the passion for spirit that surges forth from their own heart. Only remind them of who they truly are."

"But me?" I stammered. "You want me to remind them? Can't you choose someone with more talent or more ability? I get really uncomfortable if anybody even pays too much attention to me! I'm not right for this job."

"Your distaste for being the center of attention is most helpful," they answered softly. "Your work will always come from the center of your heart and not from your social mind's desire for power."

Now quietly sobbing, I heard a gentle message of comfort. "There is already one on Earth to help you, one who waits for you to find him."

Trying to pull myself together, I asked, "Who? I don't know anyone up to this task." I felt another surge of desperation.

"Please, choose another person. I don't have what it takes to help everyone remember!"

"Oh, Karen." The familiar little voice came from my left side. "Of course you do . . . besides, it's your job. It's best if you do it."

"But, Daniel, I don't even know where to begin."

"I'll help you," he said cheerfully.

"Daniel?" I cried, relief sweeping through me. "You? You'll come with me and help everyone remember? Thank God. I can't do this by myself."

"Of course I will," he replied with a joyful laugh.

"But not just me." Waving me forward, he added, "Come this way. There's somebody you have to meet."

❧ THIRTY-FOUR ❧

Filled with brilliant light, a long staircase descended as far as I could see. Gathered on either side, a multitude of luminous figures greeted us with gentle smiles and outstretched arms. Beautiful particles of purple, silver, and blue drifted within them. Their clear blue eyes sparkled with love.

Compelled by something unknown, I began to move down the steps. Reaching out to touch me as I passed by, a thousand incandescent beings welcomed my arrival. I didn't know what lay at the bottom of the magical stairs. But in the presence of limitless love, there was nothing to fear.

I knew before she touched me that she was mine. A magnificent being draped in moving silver light, she greeted me with her eyes long before I came to her place on the stairs. All around her, tiny spheres of yellow and palest blue spun and sparkled like drops of dew shaken from a rose petal.

"Hello." Carried on a whisper, the simple word landed in my heart and filled it with love.

"I'm glad you have come," she continued, now turning to accompany me down the staircase.

"Are you my soul?" I asked softly.

"No, my dear one," she replied with a gentle laugh. "I am not your soul."

"Who are you?" I didn't fear her answer.

"Oh, in good time you'll see," she said, wrapping her energy around me. Instantly comforted, I stayed beside her, each step down increasing my sense of safety.

After a long while, she stopped and turned toward a shimmering wall of violet light. "Here. This is where we need to go," she said as she walked straight through the splendid boundary.

Not wanting to be left behind, I stretched out my hand and touched the light. Instantly, my body was pulled through to the other side.

My new companion smiled and began to grow. Spreading her light across a deep and empty space, she was soon as large as a maple tree. Standing at her feet, I looked up into her glimmering face and waited for instruction.

"Come here," she called sweetly. With her invitation, my heart opened to whatever she wished of me, and I found myself sitting very near her beautiful face.

Looking down from my new vantage point, I could see that she held something in her cupped hands. Slowly turning, a transparent cloud of energy melted in and out of itself, now presenting twinkling shades of pale green, now softest blue and gold.

"What is that?" I whispered, careful not to disturb the beauty before me.

A simple laugh of purest love blew past me like a tiny bell ringing in a breeze. Then she said, "Why, this is your true companion."

Stunned, I watched a cascade of sparkling light pour from her and rain down over the cloud. Instantly, the energy penetrated deep inside it, like water into a thirsty earth. The colors grew brighter and more beautiful as the rotation grew faster.

"That's a human being?" I exclaimed. "It's so exquisite!"

"This is the one who will help you," she said, carefully protecting the billowy phenomenon in her hands. Glorious light continued to move freely and smoothly within it.

"What you are seeing here," she said, "is an energy body—the energy body of a living person."

I had learned from Daniel that all individuals are really a wonderful collection of energy, surrounded by their soul. But this was so incredibly intimate. Despite everything Daniel had shown me, I had still expected the soul to be far away. "And you hold him in your hands," I stammered, overwhelmed by the tremendous love this soul had for her creation. "Do you do that all the time?"

"If I did not, he would cease to exist," she responded, carefully protecting the beauty in her hands.

The soul powers our existence on Earth. How many times had Daniel explained that to me? Without her, this being wouldn't last a second.

"He has such beautiful energy, doesn't he?" she asked, holding the twinkling cloud up higher so I could see it better. It certainly was magnificent; spinning fast, the tiny spheres of color now included red, orange, silver, and deepest blue.

"Wait a minute!" I said, feeling confused. "You called him 'my true companion.' You aren't just talking about helping people to remember, are you?"

"Oh, no," she replied. "He is meant to be your lover, and your friend. It is his destiny to support you in your work in helping human beings to remember who they truly are."

"But," I protested, "I already have a husband. We've been together for ten years. Are you telling me I married the wrong person?" Like many people, I was willing to change things about my life until it came down to something really painful. At that point, most of us slam on the brakes.

"No," she answered gently. "Your husband has had a very important role up to this time. A First Step community member, he has helped to prepare you for your destiny."

"And now . . . and now, I'm just supposed to leave him be-hind?" I cried, certain I was being asked for too much.

"Of course what you do is always free will," she replied. "But his soul created him to serve a particular purpose. This he has done well."

"But . . . but, I don't want to lose him," I offered weakly, already knowing I would sacrifice anything in order to serve the wishes of my soul.

"You must simply move into a new relationship with him," the soul said, trying to comfort me. "There is no need to say good-bye. We ask only that you change how your personalities live on Earth. Moving into alignment with your souls will only bring abundant joy."

How was I ever going to explain this to anyone? Already, the experiences I had gone through transcended anything I had ever heard about. Now I was expected to go home and tell my husband our life together had to dramatically change. And yet, I could not turn away from my destiny.

"Who is the man I am supposed to be with?" I asked care-fully, feeling like the reluctant subject of a cosmic matchmaker.

"Someone I have created to carry out the work of helping humanity to remember," she answered, pouring more glorious energy into the being she held.

"Just as my own soul created me," I whispered.

"Indeed."

My mind flooded with jarring pragmatic questions. "Where do I find him? Do I already know him? How will I know who he is?"

"We will help," the soul answered. "We have already led you to the right place on your Earth."

"Boise!" I exclaimed, disbelief widening my eyes. "He lives in Boise?"

"Yes," she replied.

"Boise?" I was still unable to believe my ears. I had always thought that people who did spiritually important work came from exotic places . . . Tibet, Peru, Nepal . . . certainly not Idaho!

Reading my mind, the soul responded. "Because human beings are so sadly unfamiliar with the energies of the soul, they have trouble imagining that spirit comes through even in ordinary surroundings. Do you know that many people did not believe Jesus because he came from Galilee?"

Searching my memory, I was struck with a statement in the Bible. "Nothing good could ever come from Galilee," I whispered.

"That is what they thought," she answered. "But spirit does not care where it is you are upon the Earth. It does not matter; we are in all places."

So, I considered silently, that's why I moved to Boise. It had been an odd decision to move away from Seattle, where I had loved living. But one day, it had felt enormously important to relocate to the small city five hundred miles inland. Leaving friends and work behind without a reasonable explanation, my husband and I arrived in Boise to search for something I couldn't define. Finally, I understood what had happened. I had been guided by my soul to Boise so that I could find my true companion.

Gazing down again into the beautiful cloud of light held with such love by his soul, I asked, "But how do I find the person who is meant to help me? Boise is small, but still, it has well over a hundred thousand people! Where do I look?"

A sudden burst of brilliant yellow light toppled me from my position near the glorious face of the soul. Spiraling downward, spectacular, shooting beams of refracted light sped past me in a dazzling display of blue, violet, silver, and gold.

A divine melody wrapped around my heart, sending waves

of ecstasy rolling through me. Now, the steady beat of a human heart embraced that melody. I knew I had fallen straight into the cloud of energy held in the hands of the soul.

The rhythm of the heart increased like a deep, resonant drumbeat, summoning fiery passion from its hiding place within me. Fully ignited, blazing urgency sped along spiraled pathways of meaning and purpose never known before, exploding in one overwhelming desire.

Fragments of indigo, crimson, and orange rose and fell around me as lips murmured a ceaseless song of adoration and unseen hands created unbearable pleasure. Now flowing in and out of one another, hearts moved back and forth, now separate, now one. Slowly, relentlessly, the fire built and finally burst with the song of creation as one being was filled with the other.

Purpose imbedded in our very being, we prepared for a sacred departure. The arms held each other, and the hearts beat in remembrance of all things shared. Eyes overflowed with joy, and the hands slowly drew apart, fingertips finally releasing with a gentle promise to find one another again.

Then, carried on a deep sigh, each one drifted into forever.

ᘓ THIRTY-FIVE ᘔ

"Hi." Daniel's voice sounded high above me. "Open your eyes." As usual, his words were infused with happiness.

"Oh, Daniel," I murmured. "I don't want to." Deep, satisfying waves of love continued to caress every part of my being.

"It's okay," he said. "Once you know that kind of love again, you never forget it."

Slowly, I lifted heavy lids to find Daniel perched on a tree branch directly over me. "Hi," he said with a grin.

"Daniel . . ." I whispered. "My God, do you know where I've been? Do you know who waits for me?"

"Yep," he replied cheerfully. "See, it's not so bad to follow the direction of your soul, is it?"

"Oh, I never even imagined such bliss," I responded, incredibly thankful for the profound guidance of the being who had created me.

Gingerly, I untangled my limbs and sat up. It appeared we were back in Boise. An expanse of grass punctuated by mature trees indicated we were in one of the city's parks.

"Daniel . . . it was all so glorious. I didn't want to come back."

"That's the point, silly," he replied. "You aren't 'back' because you didn't go anywhere. Your soul was right here all the time. That's what I keep trying to tell you."

"I can't see it all the time," I said sadly. "I know it's here, but I feel separate from it because I can't see it."

"You don't have to. You can feel it in your heart, right?"

That was certainly true. My heart sang with the newfound joy of reconciliation. Smiling softly, I said, "I have so many questions."

"Of course you do!"

"I've got to find him, Daniel," I said urgently. "I have to find his body, his personality. I have seen his soul and felt his energy." Emotion spilled over, and tears rolled down my face. "Please help me; I have to find him."

"You will," he answered cryptically.

Seeing he wasn't willing to address my foremost concern, I proceeded with my other questions. "Daniel, are there other people on Earth who have ended up with the wrong partner? I know we all make mistakes about who we choose, but from the soul's perspective, do lots of people have a partner somewhere that they are destined to be with?"

"Of course," he answered, scrambling down from the tree. "Many human beings have contracts with others."

"Contracts?" That was an odd word to use in connection with spirit. "Like legal contracts?"

"No," he said with a laugh. "Soul contracts."

"What does that mean?" I watched him begin to collect bright orange and red leaves from the ground.

"See," he said, looking over at me, "sometimes souls send their people into the Earthtime to learn special lessons that require two beings to play out. When they do, a contract is made that determines the relationship those beings will have in their lifetimes."

I was confused. "So they aren't always married partners?"

"Oh, no. Lots of times, the contract has nothing to do with marriage or even a long-term relationship. It's just an agreement made by the souls for their beings to complete particular work while on Earth."

"Is this what people call soul mates?"

"No," he replied. "Love can be found in beings all over your Earth. The idea that there is only one possible partner for any person is just plain wrong."

"It did seem like a peculiar romantic idea to me," I ventured. "It seems like a lot of people use that as an excuse to not look for or accept the possibilities for love that are around them."

"Love is everywhere," he said, grinning. "You just have to open your heart and remember—"

"Who we truly are," I interrupted. If there was one thing I had learned on this spectacular adventure, it was the desperate importance of remembering our true identity.

"So many people do not have contracts at all?" I asked, already knowing the answer.

"Nope," he said. "But remember, even if they do, that contract can be with a being who comes as a son or daughter. It can be with someone who is a special friend. It doesn't have to be a relationship with a lifelong mate."

"But I bet people feel something different when they meet up with someone with whom they have a contract!"

"Yep," he answered, spreading the leaves back out over the grass. "Like when a person feels like he's known somebody forever and yet, they've just met."

I smiled with understanding, "But the souls have known each other forever!"

"Of course!"

"But why are relationships so difficult on Earth? Is it all the social mind's ability to destroy love?"

"The social mind messes up everything," the little boy replied. "By cutting off your connection to the energies of the soul, you become desperate. Then you make all kinds of mistakes when it comes to what you call love. When you try to make another person the replacement for those essential energies, the relationship is doomed from the start."

"We end up chronically disappointed, no matter who we try to have a relationship with." I knew that feeling all too well.

"Disappointed, angry, confused, and unsatisfied," he added. "No person can ever replace the nourishment of your soul."

"So most relationships are really only two social minds competing for energy?"

"Yep," he said. "Just two social minds terrified of not having enough energy to survive."

"What else is going on?"

"The social mind confuses instructions from the communities by constantly interfering with the energies of the soul. When people don't understand the energies of their soul's community, they end up with yucky personality stuff. Then people argue because their confused understandings clash."

"Like the First Step community and the Gaia community," I said. "They judge each other from their own distorted understanding about how each of them should be!"

"Yep," he said.

"The First Step person gets relentless and humorless about what he's trying to accomplish, while the Gaia person gets even less focused and more confused. I mentally sorted through various people I had known. "Or, a Line community person tries to get everything nailed down, safe, and secure while a Healing community person desperately tries to talk to him about intimacy, love, and the need to communicate."

"That's how it works," he said perfunctorily.

"This explains so much!" I exclaimed, regretting that I hadn't been able to offer this information to the countless couples I had counseled.

"The social mind is an awful thing," Daniel added, wrinkling his face in distaste.

Outrage swept through my body. "The social mind is a terrible opponent! It's the very opposite of spirit. All it wants to do is take all our natural power away, the power we gain from the energies of the soul. All it wants is to conquer and demolish spirit wherever it goes!" I could see how destructive this false part of ourselves was. It really wasn't just a critical voice within us, but a powerful force, actively opposed to the energies of spirit.

I continued. "The social mind is what has always killed the wonderful teachers like Jesus who came to help us. And now it's attacking Gaia to the point that her body could give out entirely. All of us could be destroyed by something that takes everything subtle and beautiful, everything that is of the heart, and attacks it with a vengeance . . ." My voice trailed off as an incredible thought rose up like a tidal wave inside me. I tried to summon the courage to say it.

For centuries, we had been warned of a terrible being who would come to Earth, spreading evil wherever he went. In the final days, this person would lead people toward their own destruction. Fire would descend from the sky and kill all life on Earth, except those saved by Jesus. There were many theories about who this person might be. The current speculation pointed to someone born in the Middle East. But what I was thinking was much more terrible than that. All this time, how could we have been so blind?

Taking a deep breath, I whispered, "That's it, isn't it? The terrible being we were told to watch out for, the evil one who attacks the soul and could actually destroy the world—I know who it is. My God, Daniel, I know who it is."

꧁ THIRTY-SIX ꧂

The little child looked at me, confirming with his eyes that what I was thinking was actually true. Quietly, he encouraged me to bring it out into the open. "Go ahead, Karen. Go ahead and say it."

I squeaked out the horrible name. "The Antichrist. It isn't an actual person who will come and lead an evil attack on humanity. It's worse than that. This awful thing in the process of destroying us right now, it's not out there someplace. Daniel, it's right here, it's a part of us!"

Daniel looked soberly at me for a very long time. "Yes it is, Karen. The Antichrist lives in all of you, because you create it and feed it. The time has come for you all to decide, to make a real choice between the energies of the soul and the energies of the social mind . . . symbolized by Christ and the Antichrist."

I was horrified. "And right now, the Antichrist is running rampant, isn't it? That's what's got us. If we don't stop it, the terrible stories will end up being true. We'll be devoured by ugliness, violence, and our hatred for each other and the Earth."

"Yes," he replied.

My God, we had all been taught to watch out for this horrible thing. For hundreds of years, we had waited for this malevolent being to bring the world to an end. We had been told to "search out there"—the same behavior that had kept us lost for so long! While we were looking outside ourselves for Jesus to save us, the energies of the soul and its destroyer had both been inside us.

I needed to be sure. "This Antichrist, our own social mind, it's powerful and cunning just like they always said, but it's inside us! It isn't just some concept, it's real and it's destroying everything while we wait for something in the sky to come and save us!"

"It's been the social mind that waged the wars in the name of Christ," Daniel said. "It's the social mind that keeps you so separated from your heart that you can be horrendously violent to each other. It's the social mind that looks at the color of someone's skin and tells you they are fundamentally different from you. The social mind forms the opinions and makes the judgments that allow some of you to eat while others starve to death."

"Even in our own country, we have people living homeless on the streets! For God's sake, we have small children without anywhere to sleep!" I cried.

Daniel's face was strewn with tears. "The social mind robs energy. Then it convinces you it's all right to step over the bodies of those you judge morally unfit when they become too weak to make their way in the world."

Something appalling occurred to me. "Daniel, our churches . . . the way many of them function, aren't they just training centers for social minds?" Even at the most benign level, going to church was all about dressing up in your best clothes, putting the right amount of money in the collection plate, gossiping about what was going on with the other people there. But beyond that, it was starting to seem that there were much more dangerous things happening under the name of God.

I continued. "Several Protestant churches in Boise have outdoor signboards. I saw one the other day that read 'Love God,

Point the Way to Salvation, Dispense Justice.' Dispense justice! What in the world gives them the right to dispense justice?"

"Well," he replied, "all your other Christian churches came out of the Catholic church. It was first and they all came later."

I searched my scrambled brain. "But Martin Luther in the sixteenth century, the Reformation and all of that . . ."

"Right. That was supposed to liberate people from the hierarchical structure of the Catholic church. Through the right of succession, the priests and bishops had always told people they had direct contact with God. It was only through them that anybody else could be heard. So the Reformation was supposed to change all of that. Anybody could have the right to talk to God if they wanted to."

"But what's that got to do with justice?"

"Well, before the Reformation everybody was supposed to stay in line and be accountable to the church. After the Reformation, they were supposed to be directly accountable to God. But people began to make other people accountable to them. You know, keep an eye on each other and straighten out the sinners."

"So, you're saying that instead of the priest having so much power because he had the only connection to God, everybody was supposed to be able to do it themselves. When that happened, people started acting like priests and judging each other. Like when a parent leaves and the kids start challenging each other for control."

"Right," he replied. "At least the Catholic church had some pretty clear standards about what it was going to judge somebody about. Once that misguided power went into the hands of everybody, well, lots of people starting feeling pretty righteous and behaving in ways that were pretty painful for other people."

It was starting to make sense. "And that got projected into an even bigger and more vengeful angry Earth god."

"Yep. And everybody felt it was up to him or her to tell other people when they were being the right kind of person and when they weren't. Once they could do that, they could also tell people what horrible things God was going to do to them if they were bad. And that God out there kept getting bigger and angrier."

I had friends who came from churches with a terrifying concept of God. It seemed that most of their time was spent quoting scripture and talking about the last days in which God was going to punish everybody. I couldn't stand it. I avoided having conversations about religion with them. And yet, these frightening ideas seemed to permeate even their discussions of even the most unrelated topics.

I came back to Daniel and asked, "On what basis did people decide who should be punished?"

"Mixed-up stuff from the Bible, mostly. But it was all the social minds deciding. So the standards for judgment changed a lot, depending on what was going on with the social minds at the time. Like what year it was, what culture it was."

I shook my head. "So, it just became a bunch of social minds interpreting an already mixed-up Bible and beating each other up with it!"

"Yep. Sounds kind of funny until you realize what came of it."

"So dispensing justice really means look at what your neighbor is doing and let him know when he's disobeying God."

"Right," he said.

The headlines in my newspaper showed what that kind of thinking could lead to. "That can get really ugly, Daniel. We have people in our country who think anything they do is justified as long as they say it's in the name of God."

"I know," he said sadly. "There's an awful lot of spiritual violence in your world."

"Spiritual violence is everywhere!" Examples were flooding through my mind.

"Yes, it is. Emotional battering in the name of God, ministers frightening people with misunderstandings about the Bible, telling people they are worthless sinners who are going to burn in hell unless they obey the Lord and Master, Jesus Christ."

I remembered another church sign: "What you decide to do with Jesus now will determine what he decides to do with you later. Repent while you can." It had seemed so horrible that I hadn't even understood what it meant for a few days.

The little boy continued. "Pastors and parishioners telling people the blood of Jesus is on their hands unless they accept him as their Lord and Savior . . ."

You could hear these statements any time on Christian radio, on countless evangelical television shows, and even in church services. "Daniel, this kind of thing is said a million times all over the Earth every day."

He looked at me. "The social mind at work."

I was afraid of his reply to my next question. "Are you saying that the people who say this kind of thing are agents of the Antichrist?"

"Yes, they are."

I swallowed hard and listened as Daniel continued. "They act as destroyers of spirit by tearing people away from their souls with fear, intimidation, mixed-up teachings, and spiritual violence. They are in opposition to true spirit. They're just social minds stealing more power for themselves by scaring other people!"

"But you're not saying they are evil . . ."

He gazed at me without blinking. "Do you know what that word means, Karen?"

"No." I was surprised at myself. "Evil" was a word used all the time, but I really didn't know what it meant.

"Absence of light," he replied.

The three simple words shocked me, but caused everything to fall into place. It was all I could do to find my voice. "It just means separated from the light of the soul, stuck in the darkness of the capsule that is formed by the social mind. Evil just means that you are under the direction of the social mind instead of the spirit, doesn't it?"

"That's what it means," he answered, holding his hands out to his sides.

"And anything that promotes judgment, fear, comparison, or dependence on a wrathful deity could be considered evil because it separates you from your soul's light and keeps you locked in darkness. Oh, my God."

"Yep. Just keeps you looking outward to the opinions and judgments of the minister, the church members, and a faraway, raging God."

There were so many churches, and so many innocent people who wandered into them looking for comfort and a sense of hope. But what really happened within those walls was awful. "And while you're distracted, the social mind just grows with energy and power like an engorged mosquito."

He looked at me soberly. "And the more separated you are from spirit, the more you can justify any kind of action against another person."

I knew exactly what he meant. "Like murder."

He nodded. "Like murder, child beating, spouse abuse, racial violence . . ."

My heart was pounding with the injustice of it all. "And this is done in the name of God. It's justified because the other person is not what you think they ought to be, according to a horribly scrambled mess of a message."

"That's how it works."

I felt sick. "And it's all been a tragic misunderstanding."

Quietly he answered, "I'm afraid so."

How could we have gotten so far off track? What Jesus had come to say was so beautifully straightforward. "Jesus was just trying to tell us how to clear our density, and make our heart wheel turn with the energies of the soul. He was trying to tell us how to offer another person those energies of love, just like we would want them to do for us."

We sat together for a long while, each filled with sadness at the tragedy of it all. Mankind had been given so many wonderful teachers—Jesus, the Buddha, Mohammed—each with the very same message. And like any information that passes through different ears and different hands, what we had been left with did not make any sense at all.

I looked out across the expanse of green and saw a church in the distance. I knew its doors were probably locked today. After all, there was nothing to do in that magnificent sanctuary when Sunday services were over. But on top of that church, on a tall spire, was a white cross. And that cross was the embodiment of incredible hope. It was not hope for rescue by a supernatural being on Judgment Day, but hope for a joyful reunion with the divine that was present now and would surround me forever. I knew it was up to me to move off the horizontal, static, everyday part of that cross. I knew I would climb out of my density and live as I was meant to, one with my soul.

I heard a whisper. "With all your strength, lift your sight. Tears will fall from your eyes, and fountains of love will unleash from your heart. Shed your ignorance and look in your heart for that which knows its own lover like no other. Unfasten your joy, release your passion, push away all that holds you back, and run toward me with all you have."

I smiled through my tears and realized I had again heard the voice of my soul.

ഈ THIRTY-SEVEN ഈ

"That's so good, Karen!" Looking up, I barely had time to notice we were no longer sitting on the grass. From underneath me came a powerful force, and I was thrust violently into the air. Sparkling blue water streamed from something enormous, and I took in a huge breath as we headed down. My eyes wide open with shock, I searched below me in murky water, unable to believe my mind. Up we went, shooting forward into the sunshine, my arms clutched madly over the back of a beast.

"Daniel! Oh God, Daniel!" I screamed, frantically searching the glittering surface for help. But like a bucking bronco, the animal bent and took me under again.

"First you have to learn a different way to breathe." I heard him clearly in my tortured mind, but he was nowhere to be seen. I gripped harder as my captor took off, rushing through the water.

Suddenly, we broke the surface again and I gasped for air. Through eyes blurred with salt water, I saw pine trees along a distant shore. We must be somewhere in the north. As if that fact could provide me with an answer to my dilemma, I relaxed a little and was promptly submerged again.

"You can't help them unless you learn to breathe differently." Again the little voice spoke directly to my mind.

I silently roared, "What does that mean? Please, just tell me what you mean!"

Suddenly I sat soaking wet on shore. Shaking water off like an ungainly dog after a bath, I looked around for Daniel. Of course he was nowhere to be seen. Tall conifers hugged the cold, empty stretch of beach. Abandoned by the tide, driftwood lay scattered across the wet expanse of lonely sand.

Lifting my eyes out over the gray water, I saw a pod of whales offshore. I had never seen such a wonderful, wild sight. Astounded by their beauty, I stood up to watch one leviathan breach and then disappear. He left a dazzling, sun-filled spray of water behind.

"Hi." I turned quickly to see Daniel, dressed for the cold. Clad in jeans, red flannel shirt, boots, and gloves, he looked like he'd jumped from the pages of a catalog for outdoor gear. I, on the other hand, was still sopping wet.

"What in the world was all that about?" My voice sounded angry. My capacity for dealing with the unexpected had been depleted during the course of this miraculous day.

"Just wanted you to see," he said. From nowhere, he produced a red and black plaid blanket and held it out to me.

"See what?" I asked, clutching the luscious, soft wool around my shivering body.

"What you have to do," he said as if he expected me to know what he was talking about. Looking a little dismayed, he added, "You know, you don't have to stay cold, unless you really want to."

My trembling had slowed considerably and I answered perfunctorily, "The blanket is working nicely, thank you."

"No." He shook his head. "I mean you don't have to stay that way. Just turn up your energy."

"What?" I didn't have any idea what he was talking about. "How in the world do I do that?"

He looked exasperated and said, "Well, you can start by

asking Adam to release some of the energy through your system that you told him he should hang onto when you got scared."

"Oh." I felt silly. After all, I already knew that. It was just that I seemed to forget everything I had learned whenever I got frightened.

"Why do you suppose that is?" He read my mind.

"Because . . . because it seems like the crisis on the outside is real, and I have to forget the more subtle things in order to rally and meet it." I knew as soon as I said it that it was a ridiculous concept. I had already experienced how limiting that kind of attitude could be.

"What do you think happens then?" he asked.

"I know, I know. My social mind has a great opportunity to convince me once again that it's very important."

"Right!" He bent down and picked up a tiny broken shell, then asked casually, "So do you think that's a good thing to have happen?"

"No," I said sheepishly. "When I give it control, I lose abilities, not gain them."

"Yep," he replied, carefully putting the shell back on the sand exactly as he had found it.

Someday, perhaps I would automatically implement what I had learned. It was frustrating to see how quickly my social mind could gain the upper hand.

I gazed out to sea and, finding no further sign of the whales, asked, "Daniel, what was that all about? What happened back there?"

He began to giggle. "I just wanted you to see. I thought I'd get your attention."

I felt my irritation come back to the surface like an ugly piece of plastic someone had tossed thoughtlessly into the water. "I don't understand. If I was where I think I was, you could have gotten me killed."

He grinned back at me. "Well, it's like this. When people are stuck in their personality self, they're like barnacles on the whale. And the soul, well, it's like the whale you were just riding."

I protested loudly, "Riding! Is that what you would call it!"

Laughing, he replied, "Well, you were trying really hard!"

"Trying to save my life!" I responded adamantly, kicking up some sand with the edge of my shoe.

"Oh, Karen, I wouldn't let anything happen to you," he replied, his innocent face completely devoid of sympathy.

That struck me as an extremely inaccurate statement, given what I had experienced today. My mind had been completely shattered, for a start. But I knew it was good. It had just been incredibly painful at times.

I took in a breath of the wonderfully cleansing ocean air. "So why is that important for me to see?"

He had wandered to the edge of the water. Crouching down, he began to play with some bubbling foam left behind by a wave. "Because you want to try to help people remember who they really are, and know what?"

My irritation had ebbed, and I walked down to the water. "What?"

Standing up, he looked very serious. "Some of them aren't going to like it at all."

"They aren't?" We moved back quickly as an unexpected rush of water nearly covered our feet.

"Nope." He looked up and reminded me, "You didn't."

He was sure right about that. I felt embarrassed when I considered the spectacular things he had shown me, and how I had fought furiously against him most of the way. I was sorry I had been unable to simply embrace what he had wanted to help me experience. "That's true. I apologize."

"That's okay," he replied, patting my arm. "Unfortunately,

that's the way most people react. When you tell them about their soul, some of them don't like the idea that something is more important than who they think they are. They forget that it's all them. I mean, their soul isn't somebody different telling them what to do, it is them. It's who they really are."

I understood what he was saying. None of us like the idea that we're not as important as we thought we were. "So they end up feeling like the barnacle when the whale decides to go somewhere, kind of powerless."

He was clearly pleased with my understanding. "Yep. But that's a mistake!"

"Because they're not the barnacle, they're the whale! We're more important than we thought we were, but in a way we have to learn to understand."

"Right!" Daniel was a teacher who was most happy when his student was able to answer the questions himself.

"What did you mean when you said I had to learn how to breathe differently?" He had lost me there. What did breathing have to do with learning about the soul?

"Well," he said adamantly, "if you're going into the realm of the whale, you'd better be able to survive there and not think so much about what's being left behind!"

I nodded in agreement before I realized I didn't really understand what he was telling me. "I'm not quite sure what you mean."

"Well, it's just that when a person's capsule begins to be challenged, let alone break down, he gets kind of upset."

"Like I did," I said.

"Yep." His voice was reassuring. "Most people look outside for answers. That's why they end up so dependent on keepers and other social minds. They're used to looking to the outside world to tell them all about inside stuff. But that doesn't work at all!"

Of course it wouldn't work. Nothing anybody could tell you could compare to the experience of being out of the capsule. In fact, what most people had to say would only fill that space with more social mind clutter. I knew what it was like to be free, and it only came with a letting go. "You have to experience being out of the capsule for yourself, like I did!"

"Right." He paused, and we watched a flock of sandpipers dash madly toward the water as it receded, and then race speedily for the sand when a little wave swept ashore. He continued, "See, it's kind of like someone who paddles a boat across the seas, going from place to place, working like crazy to get somewhere to find the answers. But all the while, what they really need to do is get out of the boat and dive into the water and start for the deep."

"Going inward, not outward." That was not common in our culture. People who wanted to spend time alone were always suspect. It seemed that every time somebody committed an atrocious crime, the first thing others said was "He was always a loner."

But this wasn't about cutting yourself off from other people, it was about knowing that you had an incredible world inside yourself. Past the concerns of the day, past endless ruminations about your day, your job and your relationships, there was an amazing richness to tap into.

I remembered reading what Carl Jung said about introversion and extroversion. Even those terms evoked judgment in our culture. An introvert was some kind of social incompetent, and an extrovert was someone who was wonderfully entertaining. But Jung had described something different. He used the word "introvert" to describe someone who gained his energy from deep inside himself, and "extrovert" as a person who gained his energy from people and activities outside himself. Most of us were in the second category. Our daily life was an exercise in gathering energy from the outside so that we could go on. With that kind of reliance on the outside, we never even thought to look inside.

The little boy interrupted my thoughts. "It's not a horizontal thing, it's a vertical thing—you know, diving, not paddling!"

I was beginning to understand what he meant. "So if you're going to dive, you have to learn a different way to breathe."

"Right." Daniel picked up a long strand of seaweed and began to snap it back and forth. "When you jump out of the boat, into the inner and away from the outer, it's a change in elements. It's like going from air into water. You're going to be less in the personality and more in the realm of spirit. The rules will change."

I knew what most people would think about that idea. "Boy, I can hear social minds all over the place. 'Are you crazy? Stay in the boat! It's dangerous out there.' " Most of us did not like going into the unknown. We wanted to grow, but not change. That was impossible, but we kept trying anyway.

"Right," he said, dropping his seaweed whip. "Not only other personalities, but your own as well."

"So there's some panic and uncertainty when you hit the water, when you start looking inside yourself for answers."

"Yep," he replied, skipping a few yards away. "Confusion, fear, uncertainty . . . and other people probably won't help at all. But see, diving is a solitary thing, not a group thing. If you try to take others with you, they'll just act like buoys. They'll bring you right back to the surface."

It was true. If we did venture into the unknown, we always wanted to have company. The next thing you know, you're asking the other person about his experience, what he thinks about what you're doing. Then you get knocked off course when he inevitably has a different idea, challenges what you're doing.

"You could spend an awfully long time just paddling on the

surface, looking for another teacher, another group, another church, another philosophy."

"Lifetimes. Once you go inward, you can't see where you're going. You don't know how it works, so your personality starts trying like mad to go back where it's safe. If you look around, you don't see any other personalities diving. They're all in the boat."

"Because that's what we're taught to do from the start—stay where everybody else is." I was beginning to resent the Greek chorus in everyone's life. It constantly gives a socially correct opinion about everything you do.

"But if you stay in the water"—he paused and grinned—"you learn to breathe water. You learn to draw what you need from the inner, not the outer."

"And I bet you never learn that unless you take the plunge, so to speak."

"Nope!" he yelled, running toward the water. "Your personality doesn't want you to learn that you can live on your inner resources! Then it wouldn't have a job. It wouldn't be able to steal energy from other people and have control over everything."

"But, Daniel," I called after him. "I've seen it myself. The inner worlds are so much more beautiful than anything on the surface!"

Suddenly, he was behind me, and I jumped when he said, "Yep. But it's scary to begin with, huh?"

I thought about the multiple episodes of terror I had experienced with Daniel today. "To look at it another way, it's kind of like leaping off the ledge into the darkness. You leap before you know how to fly and kind of learn that on the way down."

"That's a good way to see it." As he opened his hand, I was surprised to see a lovely yellow butterfly. "Like if a caterpillar went off a ledge and had to become a butterfly before he hit the ground."

I watched the magical butterfly flutter away. "What would happen if the caterpillar refused to give way to the butterfly?"

"Not a pretty sight," he said, scrunching up his small face.

I was very familiar with the human character. "Most people aren't going to take a leap off into nowhere." Because of Daniel, I had been blessed with the chance to dive straight off a cliff, but most people were not going to volunteer to do the same thing. "You made me do it that way, but isn't it usually different somehow? I mean, doesn't a person have to be ready?"

He heaved a huge sigh. "People are never ready, that's the whole problem. If we wait until you're all ready, there will be nothing left!"

"I guess the time for endless meandering is about over, isn't it?" I thought about all the time I had wasted in my life trying to gear up for something uncomfortable. I had grasped at any excuse to avoid doing something I was afraid of. Nearly everyone I knew was the same way. But we couldn't continue like that. "This second chance is so important because Gaia can't go on like this forever."

"Nope." He looked down the beach, and a soft, cold wind blew his blond hair back from his face. Then he turned toward me and said brightly, "But there's a lot of extra help for you right now. The beings from upper heaven are sending lots of helpers to light the way for you to come home. But it's always got to be free will."

I thought he had said that angels weren't real. "Daniel, I thought you told me it was a waste of time to call out to angels."

"Well, it is. You have to do your own work to get out of the capsule. But that doesn't mean there isn't wonderful help for you. It's just that you can't sit around expecting something to come along and save you from what you have chosen to construct for yourself."

I picked up a gorgeous pink shell and inspected its ridged surface. Carefully, I put it back where I had found it, just as Daniel had done. "So when people say they are talking to angels or seeing angels, is that their imagination?"

"Sometimes. But sometimes it's a lot more dangerous than that."

"What do you mean?" I geared myself up for another shock of some kind.

He smiled gently, as if to comfort me in advance. "Well, you saw the personality self being absorbed back into the soul when the life on Earth ended."

"Yes," I replied tentatively.

"Going back to the soul is always a matter of free will, whether you're in the body or out of it." Playfully, he directed the searching arms of a crab in my direction before tenderly setting it down. "Sometimes the personality won't go home and it stays with the Earth."

"Like ghosts and evil spirits, that kind of thing?" I could accept that. After all, just about everyone believed in at least the possibility of haunted houses.

"Well, kind of, sort of, not exactly." He sat down on a battered log. "A lot of the time these personalities aren't bad, they're just in the wrong place. And, just like people in bodies, they have talents and limitations. The problem is, they get tangled up with the energy of people who are still living on the Earth."

I sat beside him. "Wait a minute! You're not talking about ghosts lingering in a house somewhere. Are you saying these spirits can actually hang out with a living person?"

"Sure," he said matter-of-factly. "They start giving advice and talking about stuff they really don't know anything about.

Because humans are so astounded by anything without a body, people usually assume these personalities are angels or guides with something valuable to say. But they're usually just regular personalities who don't have any more wisdom than they did when they had bodies."

People seemed obsessed with angels lately. I hadn't really known what to think. It was a romantic idea, but it had seemed too simple to me. "I hear lots of people talk about their guides and angels. Are you telling me these could just be some ordinary people who are getting a lot of attention because they're speaking without a body?"

"Yep."

"No wonder the reports about what they say are often so weird!"

"Yep. Same old social mind, just running around trying to control other people. Except it's a lot easier when people's eyes are popping out of their heads because they hear a voice without its own body. The more weird it is, the more people seem to like it."

"But there are other beings, real beings out there! I saw them myself!"

He looked at me reassuringly. "Well, first of all, there is no 'out there,' remember? It's all right here, ready for you to open to it. Karen, your own soul has everything you need. It's what each person should be looking to. It's the most important thing! But there is additional help with the process of going home."

I felt relieved. "So our own soul is really the only angel we should listen to."

He smiled. "Well, if you insist on calling it an angel, you can. Whatever you want to call it, your own soul is your only way home."

I allowed this to sink in for a moment. It made perfect sense. Why should we look for celestial beings to swoop down and save us? Wasn't that more of the same old mixed-up religious teaching? Our own soul was something much more intimate than that. It was what we belonged to. It could provide all the love and guidance we needed. I had experienced that firsthand.

"So what can people expect? I mean, if they're willing to go inward, if they're willing to go into the realm of the whale?"

He jumped off the log and began to run in a big circle. Calling out his answer, he said, "You know how the personality creates all those illusions in its little capsule kingdom? It gets drunk on its creations. It feels like the king of its world."

My eyes tried to follow him. "Yes, unfortunately, I know that from personal experience."

"Well," he said, temporarily out of breath, "when you go to the inner, all that begins to break down. You start asking, is that all there is?"

This was familiar territory. "When you've got it all and it's still not enough, you still feel empty inside."

"Yep," he replied, holding up a sand polished black stone for me to see. "The person starts to wake up. He notices that he has a whole bunch of stuff, people admire him, he drives a nice car, he looks good . . . but so what?"

I knew this feeling. And I had listened to a thousand clients express the same thing. "There's really no happiness, no peace inside. You have to beat off the emptiness every day . . . eat, drink, do drugs, keep busy, do anything to forget the fear."

"Mostly, people just work harder and do more to try to stop that fear and loneliness. After all, holing up like a caterpillar in the dark of the chrysalis and watching your legs fall off doesn't seem nearly as appealing as competing with the other caterpillars!"

"Well, when you put it that way, it really doesn't." I remembered working frantically and feeling stressed. But that was much more comfortable than when I slowed down and was quiet. Not being busy was a scary thing. I hadn't wanted to face what I was feeling inside.

"See, when the person starts to feel this way, the soul is really happy! But the personality can be really miserable. It's hard to convince people that that kind of feeling awful is really a good thing."

I stood up and stretched. "Then what happens?"

Copying me, he held his arms up high over his head. "People start to face the fact that they aren't their jobs, they aren't their relationships, they aren't their cars. And they want to know, if I'm not those things, what the heck am I?"

"And the spell of those illusions in the capsule is broken!"

"Right."

"And all the things you used to draw your identity from start to not matter so much. You're left wondering, just who am I?"

"Yep. And gradually the person lets go of what he used to think of as himself. Once he realizes that the trappings of his life aren't 'him,' he doesn't want to spend his time working so hard to keep them all. The old things don't seem as important as figuring out who he is."

"That's when all the other personalities really get upset! I tried to imagine how my friends were going to react when I began changing my life in accordance with what I had learned today."

Daniel took a few steps back and pushed his toes deep into the wet sand. "The person can't really tell people what he's feeling. It doesn't make much sense to him yet. All he knows is he's not just what's on the outside. The kingdom of the capsule is not all there is."

"So other people start sending him to counselors and doctors. They want to get him fixed, back to the way he used to be—a good, productive, predictable citizen."

All our mental health standards had to do with how well the person was able to function in society. Was he able to perform well at work? Did he dress within standard norms? Was he able to set responsible goals and fulfill them adequately? Did he get along well with others? As soon as the person got back in line, we were happy.

Daniel noticed my increasing dismay at the role I had played in keeping others trapped in their social minds. "People don't like somebody breaking out of the capsule. It makes them nervous. They'll try to get him to stop. If that doesn't work, they harden up the walls of their own capsule and call the other person selfish, or sick, or some other bad name."

"But it's really just their social mind feeling threatened!" I had always hated anything that had to do with imprisonment. The idea that I could become trapped, unable to make my own choices, had motivated me to pursue an independent career. I had deliberately stayed well away from corporate life. I had a fear of being under someone else's thumb. But the whole time, I had my own master inside who didn't want me to know there was any possibility of true freedom.

"Right." He watched me for a moment. "And you know what? Sometimes the person will get so mixed up, he'll go back to the old way of looking at things, just to please other people. And sometimes Adam will think that lifetime doesn't have any purpose anymore. Next thing you know, the body starts breaking down—illness, accidents, depression. People can just wither away."

I thought of the incredible strength of people who had broken their chains and bolted for freedom. I said quietly, "But some people will find the courage to keep going."

"Yep." He showed me another shell. It was no longer occupied, but it had once been some creature's shelter. I wondered if that life had outgrown this container and gone in search of another one. Did it have more freedom to move than we allowed ourselves?

Daniel interrupted my thoughts with a statement of hope. "Sometimes a person gets really determined to go forward and starts pushing on the walls of the capsule really hard."

"And that's wonderful!" What an incredible day of liberation that would be for any person who was strong enough to claim what was his.

I was surprised by his reply. "Well, kind of, sort of, not exactly . . . See, when the capsule begins to break down, the personality sees the end of its kingdom and gets super upset."

I should have known it couldn't be that simple. "Kind of like death throes?"

"Yep." Daniel was temporarily distracted by a rowdy seagull screaming overhead. He turned his back to me, but then continued. "So it sends up awful anxiety. Sometimes the person becomes really frantic. If his life isn't going to be what he thought it was, then what is it going to be? He wants to know that right now. And he wants to know exactly."

I walked around to face him. "And that's impossible to know because he hasn't gone far enough yet to really see anything for himself. He's just starting to break free."

"Right," he said, catching a white feather drifting on the breeze. "He can't really go back, 'cause once you see the kingdom is false, well, you can't just forget about that."

"So that's a pretty miserable stage," I said, inspecting the feather's delicate gray edges.

He shrugged his small shoulders. "Sometimes. People can have lots of symptoms, be really scared, depressed, uncertain."

From within me, the answer from my social mind found its well-practiced pathway and was immediately available. "And other personalities say, 'Aha, I told you not to go that direction. See how unhappy you are!' "

"Yep," he said. "The other social minds are really, really pleased because their people are never going to challenge that part of themselves after watching somebody else's misery."

I said softly, "But the soul is very happy with the person's progress."

"The soul is singing with joy as the pieces of the capsule fall away. It keeps sending love and encouragement. It tells the person that the way out of the pain is to keep going, to keep letting the capsule break apart."

But I knew human nature very well. "Some people won't go any farther. They'll get scared by the pain and never find what's beyond that stage, right?"

"Then they're stuck, afraid to go forward and afraid to go back. The realm of the whale is unknown, and so far, it's proven to be pretty painful. But the kingdom of the capsule has no meaning anymore."

Again, I watched the sandpipers race away from the water, then turn and run straight into it again. Human behavior was similar. "So they run around trying to get somebody outside to fix that pain. A new teacher, counselor, religion, anything."

"I'm afraid so," he replied. "If they would just keep going forward, watch for the subtlety of the soul, ask questions, and listen inside for the answers, things would be a whole lot different."

I shook my head. "We're awfully set on immediate relief, immediate gratification. That's what our culture is all about—how to do something, get something, be something as fast as possible." But now I could understand much better why it was like that. With social minds continually increasing in power, we all had to run as fast as we could just to keep up.

The little boy nodded in agreement. "Just a tool of social minds to fool you and keep the power."

My teeth ground with frustration. "It doesn't want you to

find out that all of this is just a birthing process, a reemergence into your larger self. Once you really let it all go, there is no more pain."

"Right." Daniel paused a long while. "You don't need to live in your dark little container. You don't need to remain trapped and lost and alone. You don't need to try to find freedom from your pain by going after substances, people, and things that will only divert you from it. You don't have to stay agitated and confused.

"But if you really want your freedom, you have to do something that's different from what most people would ever do. Instead of hanging on as hard as you can, you have to let go of what you think is you. And when that dies away, you are so much more than what has been lost!"

My eyes filled again at the irony of it all. "That's the paradox. What seems like the end of everything is really the beginning of everything. And you don't disappear. After all, I'm still here!"

"Yep," he said. "Your feet will remain on Gaia. But it's no longer just ground, it's the mother from upper heaven in whose arms you rest. Spirit is everywhere! It's who you are, wherever you are and whatever you do."

My face was wet with tears and salt spray. "And we've come so far. Our souls have been lost such a long, long time. Now we have a real chance to make it all the way home."

"You should honor yourselves for how far you've come," he said gently. "After all, it's been a long, treacherous journey."

I gathered myself and focused on the boundless hope for mankind that I had seen in the faces of the souls. "So if people will go through the process you just described, they can find their way out of the capsule!"

Brightly he replied, "Well, they don't have to suffer like that! Suffering isn't an essential part of spiritual growth. We see lots of people all over your Earth doing terrible things to themselves in the name of spirit. You know, beating themselves, fasting, living in awful conditions, and staying just as rigidly in their social minds as the person who lives in luxury. It's not suffering that does the trick, it's letting go. You only suffer to the degree that you refuse to let go."

I smiled as I remembered how miraculously full I had been when I allowed room for my soul. Nothing could ever compare to that feeling. "And when you let go, the soul can come flowing in."

Making room was only a sacrifice on the level of the social mind. Like ripping the wrapping paper from a Christmas present is a loss, what's inside the box is so much more! While we were stuck, unable to face giving up what we could see, we never got to the good stuff. If we wouldn't agree to change, we would never have room for anything different to come in. "Just like you told me, the soul can only enter to the exact degree that a person makes room for it."

"Yep." His face beamed with the possibilities. "When the heart opens, people can give and receive those energies of love and even use them to transform everything they touch. Love is the thing that fuels life in all the realms."

My heart was filled with hope for all of us. "We can make a conscious commitment to bring those soul energies through ourselves and right into the Earth!"

"You've all crawled forth from the same place. You've been lost for the same length of time. You've suffered in the same way, and you belong to the same home. Each person, no matter how unlikable their personality capsule might be, shares the same experience. Once your heart is opened, when your eyes meet those of another person, you will see the light of spirit shining within them. You will see right past the clothes of form."

He continued. "Once your heart is opened, you experience firsthand the reality of your true nature! You can act from the ground of who you really are, and who another other person really is, no matter what is happening at a personality level."

It was so elegantly simple. "We can become conscious, aware, and constantly in love! We begin to replace all the thick energy and darkness of density with love and light of the highest quality from the soul."

He nodded. "You can pour fresh, clean, sparkling water into a bucket filled with brown, stagnated water. The more clear and sparkling energy you pour into the dark water, the lighter the water becomes. After a while it's all clear and beautiful again."

"Daniel, it's so beautiful!" I said, happiness sweeping through me. "It's so miraculous . . . and it's been right here all along!"

The little boy stood in front of me. His chest began to shimmer and glow beneath his red shirt. That light grew and grew until radiant beams of violet, silver, and gold began to skip out across the beach.

Taking my hand, his sparkling blue eyes reflected the truth of forever. Ever so gently, his whisper caressed my heart. "Past the wounds of childhood, past the fallen dreams and the broken families, through the hurt and the loss and the agony only the night ever hears, is a waiting soul. Patient, permanent, abundant, it opens its infinite heart and asks only one thing of you . . . 'Remember who it is you really are.' "

With a soft little smile, he disappeared.

◖ THIRTY-EIGHT ◗

I heard it first. "Ladies and gentlemen, we will be landing in Seattle in approximately twenty minutes. Please begin to place your belongings back in the overhead storage compartments. The flight attendants will assist you if needed . . ."

I opened my eyes. There it all was—the 737, the passengers, my tray table with its drink. "Daniel." His name came from my mouth like a prayer, "Daniel?"

"Can I help you, miss?" A kind face appeared past the sunny voice.

"I'm not sure. I'm a little confused right now." I stumbled over my words while looking up and down the aisle for my teacher.

"I bet you had a good sleep. You were lucky to be next to an empty seat. Better get ready to land. We're almost there." With that, she walked away.

"Daniel, this isn't funny," I muttered. "Where are you?" Held back by the worried looks coming from the woman across the aisle, I stopped talking. Where had he gone this time? I knew perfectly well that I hadn't been alone on this flight, despite what the attendant had said. My heart was different. I could feel it, turning unencumbered, filled with love.

Over the stir of passengers, I heard the landing gear thud into place. The lights of the city reached up to greet us, and I wondered if anyone else realized what I knew now. How was I going to explain all of this to anyone? An unspoken shout reverberated in my head: "It's not really the way it seems to be!"

We arrived at the gate, and I followed the rest of the people off the aircraft. Searching constantly, I saw no sign of the child. Stepping out into Seattle's soft drizzle, I hailed a cab. Hoping to see Daniel just once more, I looked across the confusing buzz of people and cars. Finding nothing, I climbed inside and sank back into the seat.

"Where to?" the driver asked.

"Sheraton, downtown," I answered quietly.

The rain was harder now, sending little rivers down the windows and turning the world outside into a blur of colors. Closing my eyes for a moment, I thought about how much Daniel had given me in such a short time. I had never even had the chance to thank him.

My hands rested over my awakened heart, and I gratefully remembered all I had experienced. Lost in my feelings for a minute, I suddenly realized the taxi hadn't moved. Slowly opening my eyes, I was astounded to find the little boy sitting behind the steering wheel. Turning, he grinned and said, "Now what do you want to do?"

"Daniel! Daniel, thank God you're here!" I cried, leaning forward in my seat to touch his shoulder.

"Of course I'm here!" he replied brightly. "Where else would I be?"

I looked back at him in amazement and reminded him, "You do have a habit of disappearing!"

"Only when you don't know how to look," he said with a giggle.

"Are you trying to tell me you don't go anywhere?" I shook my head in disbelief. "It's just me who sometimes can't see you?"

The familiar peals of laughter rang out in the cab. Tears

began to fall down his sweet face with the humor of it all. "Silly! Of course I don't go anywhere!"

Despite everything he had taught me, that thought had never occurred to me. Of course he didn't go anywhere; that was the point. He had tried to get it through my head from the beginning. There is truly no separation except that which we create ourselves.

The unnerving prospect of a little boy driving through the streets of Seattle intruded on my consciousness. "Wait a minute! Daniel, are you going to drive? Where are we going?"

"That's up to you." His young face showed a determination not to make things easy for me.

"I don't know what to say." I struggled for a moment with the possibilities. All I could think of was not allowing him to drive. "Where do we go from here?"

He looked a little exasperated. "Well, you can go back or you can go forward. That's not too hard to figure out."

A tremendous resolve exploded in my heart, "Of course I don't want to go back! I want to keep going forever!"

"Are you sure?" he said with a challenge in his voice as he turned his back to me.

"Of course I'm sure!" I said, as a new thought penetrated my mind. "You have more to teach me, don't you?" Please let that be true, I pleaded silently.

I wanted to continue to grow, to reach beyond my capsule, to be free from it forever. I wanted to hear the voice of my soul all the time and bask in its love without interruption. I wanted to bring those energies to Gaia as an offering to her boundless patience. And which soul community was mine? I needed to learn about what I had sensed beyond upper heaven. Where had the voice come from? And . . . just who was Daniel?

"Lots more!" he replied happily.

I was filled with hope. "And you're coming with me to help

everyone remember where they come from and who they truly are?"

"Yep," he said with a grin.

Now I was smiling with excitement. "You're going to let other people see you! That will help a lot. They won't have to just believe me, they'll be able to see for themselves!"

Daniel grew somber. "I am everywhere, Karen. It's only density and the overwhelming voice of the social mind that blocks awareness of spirit. Those who do the work of clearing all that clouds their abilities will have no difficulty seeing what you have seen."

My enthusiasm faded. "But most people haven't done that work! They don't even know how to start! They won't be able to hear you or see you!"

"We'll help," he answered comfortably. "Until they can see for themselves, I'll just speak through you."

I wasn't sure I had heard him correctly. He must mean I would have to figure out a way to convey what he said to everyone else. It would be a little clumsy, but I would just have to listen very carefully and repeat everything exactly as I heard it. Like a speaker at the United Nations, he would need an interpreter. I could do that.

His next words shattered my comfort. "If you're willing to step outside your body once in a while, I'll just use your voice to teach them how to clear up their density and remember who they are. Pretty soon they'll hear the voice of their own soul and they won't need me anymore."

"Step outside my body?" I repeated shakily. What in the world did that mean?

"Sure," he said confidently. "You can do it if you want to. Each time I want to help, I'll just ask you to step aside. You don't have to. You can always say no."

My knees began to quake. "But . . . but where will I go? Where will I be?"

He gave me a familiar look. Of course I already knew the answer to my own question. I whispered, "I'll be in the arms of my own soul."

"Yep. And when I'm finished teaching, you'll come right back into your own body."

I was trying to cope with my anxiety. "Daniel, why don't you just create your own body? I mean, people are going to have a pretty hard time with this. Can't you just use your own body?"

"That would take too much time," he answered quietly. "Gaia needs help right now. Humanity needs to begin doing the work of liberating itself from the social mind right away."

"Oh." I silently said a final good-bye to anything resembling a normal life. Helping everyone to remember the incredible love that surrounded them in every moment was a sacred task. What lay ahead was impossibly uncomfortable to contemplate from the level of my personality. But I couldn't refuse. How could I even begin to live with myself if I turned my back on those who sought to help us all? It was excruciating to even consider keeping what I had learned to myself. It hadn't been shown to me for my private growth, but for the progress of all humanity.

My experiences had been absolutely real. I had no question about that. Any reservations I had about sharing them were coming from the closed heart of my social mind. My practice would probably vanish with the quiet judgments of those who would believe I had gone crazy. My friends and family would wonder about my mental health. But somewhere in Boise, Idaho, there was a man waiting for me to find him. We had the same job to do. He would have to believe me. And together, we would find a way for anyone who wanted to learn from Daniel to have that opportunity.

I had to have faith that some people would be willing to listen. And if they did, I knew Daniel would ignite a passion for spirit deep within their hearts. He would fan each tiny flame until it burst forth in glorious freedom. Once people heard the voice of their own souls, they would never doubt the existence of spirit. Once they knew the exquisite caress of the one who had made them, they would not need us anymore. In that, I found great comfort.

Overwhelmed with a wave of courage, I cried, "Well then, let's get to it!"

I could see the little boy in the overhead mirror, and a smile crossed his face like the rising sun. His voice full of admiration, he said softly, "I told them you would want to do it!"

With that, the cab disappeared and we sped, parting glimmering seas of silver light, straight for my soul. And again, there was no "Karen," but only the bountiful, ecstatic love of everything that is. Together, we looked out across the Earth and saw human beings everywhere, trapped inside their lonely capsules. And our heart wept tears of grief for their choices to remain separate and frightened. And with all the longing the heavens held, we sent out the cries of a million years: "Do not be afraid, for we are with you always."

But even as people remained closed, the soul patiently surrounded each one. It floated beautifully around them, a diaphanous, love-filled being of wondrous, pulsing energy. And sometimes that soul was allowed to make its way into the heart. Then that heart would begin to turn, spinning with glorious waterfalls of light. When it did, everything around it would begin to awaken and heal, shrugging off its mottled prison and searching for its deepest desire.

Gaia breathed beneath me, and I saw her heart wheel sending spectacular torrents of love through all creation. I heard her singing to her children and whispering encouragement to each one. From her noble trees and mystic mountains, from the delicate flowers swaying in a morning field, in the voice of the wind and the cry of a bird, she had forever called the same message:

"Keep going . . . do not be afraid . . . never give up . . . your home is within sight . . . only open your heart once more."

◖◖ AFTERWORD ◗◗

"Are you okay?" The deep, male voice sounded very far away. "Ma'am? Are you all right?"

Shooting down into my body, I struggled to reply. Forming words seemed impossible. Why should I have to speak? Surely, anyone could read my mind.

Slowly, fields of wavering energy solidified into recognizable shapes. A concerned skycap hovered over me. In front of us, people scurried to unload the luggage from their cars. Their strange sounds gradually settled into decipherable sentences.

"Yes," I mumbled. "Thank you. I'm all right." I was sitting on a cold, cement bench outside the terminal. "Am I in Seattle?"

"Yes, you are," he replied. His voice was kind and still concerned. "Are you sick? Do you need help?"

That was a reasonable question. A normal person would know what city she was in.

"No." I stood up and tried to regain my composure. "Thank you. It was a strange flight. I'm okay."

"Do you need a cab?" he asked, reaching out a steadying hand.

"Yes, please."

Where was I supposed to go? My original destination seemed totally inappropriate. "Daniel," I muttered. "I know you're here. What do I do now?" There was no answer. Gathering up my belongings, I stumbled into a taxi.

I wanted to go home. Not to Boise, but to the arms of the souls which had given me such boundless love. But the taxi driver waited for my instruction. Didn't he know where I had been? Didn't he understand that this visible world of cars, buildings and people was only a tiny, confusing part of an enormous reality? Of course he didn't. Nobody seemed to comprehend what waited for all of us.

"Daniel," I pleaded softly. "Come on. Talk to me. Where do I go now?"

The silence told me I needed to figure it out for myself. That had been Daniel's message all along. No one was going to come and give me answers whenever I got stuck. I had free will. I could ignore all that I had been shown, or I could go forward and create a new life for myself. I had a responsibility to share my experiences with others who might want to do the same.

In that moment, I made a firm decision that would change my life. I found my way back to Boise, and after a short period of isolation, began to tell others about what had happened to me. Predictably, I met with a variety of responses. My husband tried hard to be supportive, but was deeply concerned about my mental health. Some of my friends began to back away. A few people avoided me altogether.

Soon, I stopped talking about Daniel. Instead, I began to write about what had happened. I did not hear from Daniel for several months. Yet, wherever I went, I felt him near me. Sometimes, I could even see the briefest glimmer of the energy of a soul surrounding another person. I had a profound sense of peace. But I also felt an urgency to find a way to tell others about the miracles of spirit.

In January 1991, I saw an ad in the local newspaper about a talk to be given by a hypnotherapist who specialized in eating disorders. I felt a strange compulsion to attend the lecture, even though I had years of experience in the field and felt no need to augment my training. Driving to the auditorium, a sense of euphoria and excitement, even joy swept through me.

As soon as Rick Boyes appeared in front of the audience, I knew he was the man that Daniel had told me about. As he spoke, his soul appeared to me and gave its confirmation and blessing. Rick was my true partner—the lover, friend and companion I had seen in my travels with Daniel.

After the lecture, I went up and introduced myself as a fellow professional. Rick's blue eyes sparkled with the energies of his soul, even though his personality self had no idea about who I was or what his work on Earth was to be.

To say that it was profoundly difficult to tell Rick about Daniel and his role in helping others to receive Daniel's message would be a colossal understatement. Thankfully, it wasn't long before Daniel decided to speak to Rick. As he had promised, Daniel appeared one day and asked to use my voice to share his message. While I rested in the arms of my soul, Daniel began to teach Rick about his work on Earth. Once Rick felt the absolute love and unwavering compassion of this great spirit, he embraced his mission and we were on our way.

Since that time, hundreds of people have had the opportunity to learn from Daniel. He has remained constantly available, teaching people how to connect with their own souls, and wishing them well on their way. He does not want to become another "keeper of the buildings," but to unscramble religious confusion. His message has changed lives, created healing in minds, bodies and hearts, and inspired people to begin to find their way home.

I no longer have a counseling practice, but dedicate my life to providing Daniel with a voice so that others may hear him. I spend my time traveling with Daniel into the realm of the soul and sharing the information and experiences with anyone who wishes to listen. I continue to record my adventures, and will offer them in future books. Each person I meet is no longer a simple personality, but a wondrous, shimmering soul offering immeasureable love. Gaia supports me with her bounty and gives me the strength to do my work. I am constantly encouraged about the destiny of humanity as I receive continued instruction from Daniel, and watch those who choose to implement that teaching make miraculous connections with their own souls.

Rick and I have formed The Foundation for Spiritual Training, which acts as a clearinghouse for tapes and videos of Daniel and sponsors workshops for those who are ready to take the most exciting journey of all—the one straight into the heart of the soul.

Receive your own gift from Daniel!

When you order two or more cassette albums we'll include a complete set of **Remember Who You Are** inspirational cards free of charge.
Offer expires 12/31/97.

To Place Your Order

By Phone
Call Toll Free (800) 359-4492
Please have your Visa or MasterCard ready.

By Fax
Print your name and shipping address along with your Visa or MasterCard number and expiration date.
Fax to (208) 345-1927

By Mail
Please make your check payable to
The Foundation for Spiritual Training.
U.S. funds only please. Be certain to include
postage where applicable.
For Visa or MasterCard orders
be certain to include expiration date.
Mail your order to
967 E. Parkcenter Blvd., Suite 306, Boise, ID 83706

All orders are sent via UPS ground or US Postal Service.
Add $12 to any order for 2nd-day air.
Foreign orders must triple postage.

Healing Your Body
Contacting Your Own Nature Spirit

"And Nature Spirit spins forth a body for your sojourn
upon this earth . . ."

—*Daniel*

Align your health with the original blueprint from your soul.
Learn how to move into natural mind and communicate
directly with your own nature spirit!

Cassette Album #AP103 $49.95 plus $4 s/h

Remember Who You Are

"The lifetime which you live is meant to be in service
to highest self."

—*Daniel*

Put Daniel's teaching at your fingertips.
Stay focused on your spiritual path throughout the day with
Daniel's heartfelt inspirational messages
illuminating the journey home.

Card Set #DCards $12 plus $3 s/h

Daniel's Journal

"So we wait, we open the door, we send a teacher and extend
the hand. And you must decide what you wish to do . . ."

—*Daniel*

Receive Daniel's latest teachings with your subscription to this
inspiring quarterly publication. You will also stay abreast of
all new opportunities offered through The Foundation for
Spiritual Training.

#DJS Annual subscription $34 postage paid

Karen Alexander is the director of The Foundation for Spiritual Training, which provides continuing opportunities to learn from her spiritual guide, Daniel, through tapes and retreats. She holds a master's degree in Clinical Psychology from the Fielding Institute, and a second master's degree in Public Administration from the University of California. She has had her own counseling practice for the past seventeen years. Karen lives in Boise, Idaho, with her husband, Rick Boyes.